It's okay to cry

THE GENTLE WAY TO
DISSOLVING DEPRESSION

BRONTE SPICER

It's Okay to Cry: The Gentle Way to Dissolving Depression
© Bronte Spicer, 2021
www.brontespicer.com

Let me be clear. I'm not a doctor, psychologist, counsellor, or psychiatrist. I'm a woman who dissolved a twenty-year bout of depression. I am a mother of three gorgeous children, and wife to a beautiful man. I am a teacher, author, mindfulness mentor, sacred space holder, intuitive guide and retreat alchemist. As a Certified Kiloby Inquiries Facilitator, I teach others how to befriend their thoughts and feel their feelings using a set of advanced mindfulness techniques called the Kiloby Inquiries.

The information in this book is for educational purposes only and is not intended in any way to be a replacement for, or substitute to qualified medical advice, diagnosis or treatment, or as a replacement for, or substitute to psychological advice, diagnosis or treatment, or therapy from a fully-qualified person.

Should you have medical concerns, please seek independent advice. As you read my story and learn the techniques I used to dissolve my depression, should it raise any concerns for you, please seek advice from a mental health professional or call Lifeline on 131114.

If you think you are suffering from a medical or psychological condition, consult your doctor or other appropriately qualified professional or service immediately.

I am a Kiloby Inquiries Facilitator and not a physician, mental health or addictions counselor. I do not give advice about how to live one's life. I do not employ psychological techniques to improve one's thinking, personal story or belief systems.

What I aim to do is assist people in seeing through their identity, not constructing or changing it, as mental health counselors or therapists do.

This book is a memoir and guidebook. It reflects my recollections of experiences over time. Some names and characteristics have been changed, some events have been compressed, and some dialogue has been recreated. As the author and publisher, I hereby exclude all liability to the extent permitted by law for any errors or omissions in this book and for any loss, damage or expense (whether direct or indirect) suffered by a third party relying on any information contained in this book.

All rights reserved. No part of this publication may be reproduced, distributed or transmitted in any form or by any means, including photocopying, recording, or other electronic or mechanical methods, without the prior written permission of the author, except in the case of brief quotations embodied in critical reviews and certain other noncommercial uses permitted by copyright law. All permission requests are to be directed to the publisher using the address below.

ISBN: 978-0-6452678-0-8

Book cover design: **Ellie Schroeder**
Light code art: **Debbie Hall**
Printed on demand and distributed by **IngramSpark**

Published by **Bronte Spicer**
brontespicer@gmail.com

Acknowledgement Of Country

I want to acknowledge, thank, and hold my love for the Dja Dja Wurrung speaking people of the Kulin Nation for tending to, loving, and caring for this sacred land on which I write. I acknowledge and thank all Aboriginal and Torres Strait Islanders for being the most devoted, connected and dedicated caretakers of this land we call Australia. I offer my deepest condolences to the traditional custodians of this land for the raping of Aboriginal women, separation of families, stolen children, murders, massacres of whole communities, obliteration of sacred sites and atrocious disruptions to the delicate nature of the land since the European settlement in 1788. I trust that as we come together and listen, we can find a new way and live in harmony. With an open heart, I express my deep love for our Earth mother herself. For offering the most abundant medicine, magic and beauty. Thank you for gifting us with your raw elements for us to be nourished, thriving, clear and connected and for holding the space for us to know ourselves as free, peaceful and incredible human beings.

"Captivating and relatable. It left me wanting more."
K. Reavley

"Vulnerable and powerful."
D. Gale

"This is the book the world needs right now."
S. Hardy

" I wonder how my life may have been different if I had read this book as a young woman."
A. Goodfellow

For Jackson, Ivy, and Maggie, may all of your dreams come true.
For Mum, who did everything for me when I thought I couldn't do anything.
For Elizabeth, in loving memory of your daughter Holly.

Contents

Foreword	11
Introduction	19
Chapter One Deep Rest	29
Chapter Two Deficiency	47
Chapter Three Triggers and Trauma	61
Chapter Four What We Resist Persists	81
Chapter Five Befriending The Mind	97
Chapter Six Body Intelligence	119
Chapter Seven Clearing The Roots	145
Chapter Eight Holding Space	167
Chapter Nine Dreaming a New Dream	181
Chapter Ten Integration	195

Foreword

When we were growing up, neither our parents nor anyone else in the world explained or demonstrated to us how to truly feel our feelings. We can't really blame our parents for this any more than we can blame their parents or their parents. We've all been doing it, all humans, apparently since at least the dawn of language... and probably before.

We do learn how to think about, analyse or label our emotions. Most of us were involved in an education system that was very focused on teaching us a label or a name for everything in the world, including for every emotion that we might experience. At first glance, this learning of language for emotions may seem like the answer to our emotions. We presume, if we can think about, talk about and even understand what we're feeling, surely we can bring about a better feeling or let go of negative feelings. What we come to learn in life as we grow up is something else entirely. Most of us learn that thinking about, analyzing and labeling our feelings really isn't the answer. That may help us at certain moments, just to take the edge off of things, but most of the time when we're analyzing or thinking about our feelings, we are actually making them worse.

When we're thinking about analyzing or labeling our emotions, our focus is in the mind in our thoughts. When our focus is in our mind almost exclusively, we don't have any attention in our inner body. And yet, our inner body is exactly where we feel all emotions. As Bronte mentions in her book, even if we get to therapy, therapy is quite often focused on encouraging us to talk about our feelings. Anywhere and everywhere we look in the world, we find the same message; feelings are meant to be thought about, not felt. And yet we all know that at a very common sense level, that doesn't make any sense.

We know this but because we are conditioned so strongly to be in our heads about our feelings, this wisdom within us gets buried. When we are not directly feeling our feelings and instead thinking about, labeling or analyzing them, a whole host of issues can occur as a result. One of those issues is depression.

Bronte Spicer does an exceptional job of speaking about depression in a way that anyone could relate to. In this book, Bronte gives you her experience. She's not just telling you about her pain. She's giving very direct instructions on how to dissolve depression, the gentle way, as she says.

When I first started putting this work out into the world fifteen years ago, I had no idea how many thousands of lives would be touched by it. And not just touched by it, healed by it. The Kiloby Inquiries are bringing astonishing results to our clients at The Kiloby Center for Recovery and all around the world. The Kiloby Center is the first substance abuse treatment center in the U.S. to focus primarily on mindfulness. Independent research showed of the 76% of clients who reported trauma when they arrived, only 12% reported those symptoms when they left, 70% of clients arrived at the centre with anxiety symptoms and 3% reported those symptoms when they left and 73% of clients reported depression when they arrived while 9% reported those symptoms when they left.

The work that I do in the world is the same work that Bronte Spicer does in the world. She is an amazing certified facilitator of the Kiloby Inquiries which were co-developed by Dan McLintock and I. I sit in this wonderful position of training people in this work and then watching them blossom, watching them literally transform the world one person at a time or even one child at a time.

You may have read other books about depression. I can guarantee you've never read a book like this - that is so honest, so straightforward and so simple. In fact, the answer to depression has been right under our nose the whole time. Or more specifically right down in our stomach and chest. But we've been so busy up in our heads that we've lost touch with this simple, basic fact and therefore we've lost touch with true healing.

In fact, tons of books, millions and millions of pages of intellectual and clinical language have been written about the subject of depression. I work in the clinical field. I see it every day. Even the topic of depression has gone to our heads. In other words, we train clinicians to know a lot of information about depression, to understand all the signs and symptoms, and to even be able to diagnose depression in many cases and or prescribe treatment or medication. But in the rush, to use all those fancy words to describe the depression, something vital is missed.

In fact, something is missing in the entire mental health model throughout the whole world, as far as I can tell. This missing piece is so simple that, of course, it would be easy to miss and we have missed it every time throughout history by going back into our minds to think about our feelings, our mental health issues, and to just stay in the analysis of it, stay in the story of it. The one missing piece is to come down and to feel that from awareness directly.

I remember first hearing Bronte's name in my facilitator program. Someone told me a story of a woman from Australia who had been depressed for many years and who had tried so many different things. And she found that the simple act of coming down and feeling her feelings directly through these inquiries changed her life. I was eager just to learn more about this woman. Once she was certified, I noticed her all over social media, so much energy, so much enthusiasm and inspiration around the topic of depression. I've been doing this long enough, training people in mindfulness-based work to know when someone truly experiences transformation.

Frankly, those who have been transformed the most by my work aren't the kind of people that would just come back to me and try to convince me that they're transformed. No, they have bigger fish to fry. Their transformation is so life changing that they feel called to take this work to the world, and that's exactly what Bronte has done. Not only has she brought this to her native country and to the world, but she's brought this material to you in a simple, digestible form.

This book could help millions of people. It's that direct and instructive. When I read Bronte's book, I felt like I was learning new information. That's how incredibly concise and clear this book is on dissolving depression. Of course, I know all of these concepts; these are not new concepts to me. But they are delivered by Bronte in such a fresh manner that I'm intrigued. It's as if I'm learning about it for the first time. I can just imagine how much you, the reader, will get from this book, if I got this much from it as a co-developer.

I invite you to take this book very seriously in your life. If you've been struggling for years or even decades with depression or similar issues like trauma or anxiety, this book could be the key that you've been missing. Bronte delivers the concepts in our work in such a straightforward way, they're easy to understand in the way that she has laid them out for you in this book. I also invite you to read this book slowly. In other words, read a paragraph or two and sit back, rest in your chair or lie in bed and truly soak in the words and what they're pointing to.

This is a book of transformation. With a new book, with a book of true transformation in your hands, you want to take your time with that, marinate in it, glean from the words how to relate to your own experience in a way that is truly transformative, that moves you out of your stuck points, helps you let go of the stories in your mind that have been haunting or even torturing you emotionally for years.

I've reviewed quite a few books through the years, many of which were written by facilitators that I certified in my own mindfulness programs. This is certainly one of the best. I'm always inspired by enthusiasm that I feel coming from the pages of a book, coming literally from the being of the author. That is always inspiring to feel that enthusiasm. But enthusiasm isn't enough for me and it shouldn't be for you. What we need now here on Earth is true transformation. It's not enough to give motivational talks anymore about mental health or any other issue, we have to go deeper than that. We even have to go deeper than talk therapy or talking about our feelings.

Now it's time to feel our feelings. And Bronte is giving you the key to that in this book. Let me clue you in on a little known secret; many people already believe that they are feeling their feelings, but they aren't. They're thinking about them. As I said earlier, the transformation in this book comes from understanding and experiencing what it's like to actually feel an emotion directly. That is what makes this book so transformative.

It's not as simple, though, as just come down and feel sometimes. Inquiry is needed in order to allow the mind to come to rest enough so that you can bring attention to the body. Bronte describes that process of inquiry very clearly so that you can literally learn it from just reading the book. You could also work with Bronte in a one-on-one session, and I would highly suggest that. But this book in and of itself could change your life.

Bronte says in the book that it took her multiple years to even learn how to safely feel her feelings. It is not a coincidence that she experienced depression throughout some or all of those years. That's exactly what I see in my clinical work and in my sessions with people all over the world. Not knowing how to feel our feelings directly can result in a whole host of mental health issues, and according to modern science, some physical health issues. But as Bronte says in this book, you don't have to wait as long as she did. In fact, you don't have to wait any longer at all, you now have this book. There's a particular passage in Bronte's book on page 157 which reads as follows;

When we lose the need for the sensation to leave, we welcome, love and accept ourselves just as we are, including the sensations. The sensations are a part of us. When we allow the sensations to be in the body, we can feel safe in our skin. There is nothing from which to escape. They are just sensations. They are feelings; things you can feel in the body. When we welcome them, there is no problem.

This is just one of the many examples of simple, concise, straightforward wisdom in this book. The great thing is, these bits of wisdom are not just written about. Bronte gives you specific instructions on how to love and accept yourself just as you are, including the sensations that are uncomfortable.

I was bullied ferociously as a kid in school for months. I know exactly what Bronte is talking about at the beginning of Chapter Nine, Dreaming a New Dream. It's not just our incapacity to feel and welcome sadness that sometimes results in depression. When I was growing up, I didn't learn how to feel any feeling, and during the time that I was bullied, I was not just afraid, I was angry. Not only could I not share those feelings, I didn't even know how to feel them in a way that I could let go of them. And so I held on to that anger for decades. This led to a severe drug addiction and eventually to chronic physical pain.

The work that you are about to do for yourself, and or for your children, in this book is not just about feeling better. This is about overall mental, physical and spiritual well-being. This is about not holding on to these emotions, letting them fester in our bodies for decades, creating all sorts of health issues for us. Bronte's achille's heel was depression. Mine was addiction and chronic pain. Yours may be something different. Chances are you relate to Bronte's talk of depression, and that's why you picked up this book.

It doesn't matter what feelings or thoughts are plaguing you. This book gives you a direct path into feeling those feelings, not repressing them, not holding on to them, but also not trying to escape them anymore. Had I had this book when I was in sixth grade, it most likely would have transformed and changed the course of my life.

As Bronte shares at the beginning of Chapter Nine, if kids can't share their anger, it doesn't cease to exist. In fact, we've heard that depression can be thought of as anger turned inwards. If in some cases, depression is anger turned inward, then it's time for us to learn how to feel and share our anger. And Bronte gives you step by step instructions for that. And for the feelings of any and every emotion so that you're no longer holding on to repressing or trying to escape them.

I think this book would be wonderful for parents and children to read together and discuss. I think this book would be very helpful as part of the regular curriculum in every school. Kids can relate to it because it doesn't have a lot of fancy clinical or scientific knowledge. Parents can relate to it because it finally gives them practices that bring about transformation. And it's easy to explain to your children. I see this book as a resource to not only help individuals but also to heal families and entire communities. The world can heal by paying attention to what Bronte Spicer has to say.

I leave you in the more than capable hands of Bronte Spicer. Now it's time for you to take responsibility for your own pain. And in taking that responsibility true transformation can begin now. Don't treat this as just another book to read and place on your shelf. This book is much more than a cocktail party conversation. This book can be the key to transformation for you and your family. Keep this book handy. Refer to it often. You now have the missing piece that you've been looking for.

Scott Kiloby,
Author of Natural Rest for Addiction
www.kiloby.com

Introduction

> *What does it mean to depress something? Push down. What gets pushed down in depression? Feelings and emotions. Why would a person push down their feelings? Because they're too painful. They're too much to bear. Pushing down their feelings becomes a coping mechanism in an environment when you're not allowed to feel because your feelings threaten your attachments. So you learn to survive by pushing down your feelings and fifteen years later you're diagnosed with depression.* - **Gabor Maté**

It's easy to be overwhelmed with the world right now. There's a lot going on. As I write this, we're in the middle of a pandemic; a worldwide state of survival. In Australia, we're recovering from some atrocious bushfires. The social framework is in desperate need of repair, with domestic violence and mental illness at an all-time high. Sacred sites across Australia keep being obliterated for more roads, mining, fracking and 'economic growth'. And then there's climate change; the impending doom we feel when the people in power neglect to care for our greatest resource.

If life has been getting you down, I get it.

In 2006 at age 23, one of my deepest, darkest moments of depression, had me sitting in my room in my mess. Physically, mentally, and emotionally, I was spent. I sat on my crumpled bed surrounded by rubbish. Clothes strewn everywhere. Chocolate wrappers and empty Twisties packets had decorated my room. Positioned next to me was a jammed-full washing basket.

I'd barely been holding myself together for work. I certainly wasn't socialising. And tending to my basic personal needs was difficult. Putting a load of washing on was my mission of the moment. It felt like a marathon. Picking up the load of washing. Walking it down the stairs. Putting the clothes in the machine. Bending down to add the powder. Pressing the buttons. Walking back up to my room. It was an enormous task.

Alongside that mission was running commentary in my head about how ridiculous this was that I was having so much trouble doing something so simple. Something that people just do without thinking about it. In my mind I imagined the looks from my friends and family if they saw me struggling to put on a load of washing. *What a loser*, I heard in my head.

Avoiding the task altogether seemed so much more pleasing. I could just lay in bed instead. Except I had no clean clothes for work.

I had pep-talked myself to put the load on. 'Come on, Bronte. You can do this. Pick up the basket and put one foot in front of the other.' Memories of Mum revved me up to keep going. Step by step, I put on that mother$%&@ing load. And when I reached the top of the stairs and returned to my bedroom chaos, I fell onto the bed exhausted. After all, I had just run a marathon.

Maybe you can relate to this. Maybe you have depression. Or maybe it's your friend or family member who's stuck in this horrible turmoil. Or perhaps you're a mental health professional who wants to learn more about the best ways to meet and treat your clients.

This book is for all of you. But I will be speaking specifically to you, the person with depression. Whoever you are, wherever you're from, whatever your age, I see you, love you and respect you for being here. You are showing courage on the daily to be here, to show up.

As you read this book, we are in conversation. You're welcome to be depressed. You're allowed to be sad. Negative. Emotional. Overwhelmed. And feel like you're losing hope. In fact, I honour you for saying how you really feel and expressing how it really is. Know you're in the perfect place. You're right where you need to be. Because I'm going to show you what unravelled my depression and how it can unravel yours too.

First, you don't need fixing. This might come as a surprise to you. Maybe you've had people around you try and change you for a very long time. You don't need to change any part of you. You might just be like I was, not having been shown some fundamental skills to be human. Plus, you might not have stumbled upon the incredible intelligence you have within you to improve your mental health, and thrive.

Maybe you feel like there is something wrong with you.

Let me guess. You've tried talking to someone or attempted cognitive-behaviour therapy. Maybe you've tried mindfulness, positive thinking or raising your vibes. Has it taken your depression away?

I tried all of these. I felt peaceful and even blissful in meditation but got battered and bruised when I was back facing the challenges of everyday life. Flipping beliefs from negative to positive worked for the short-term, yet before long the negative thinking came flooding back to haunt me. I couldn't make the horrendous thinking stop coming back. Across two decades I had experienced depression and had spent countless hours in talk therapy[1] with psychologists and counsellors. While I gained some clarity and felt somewhat better, this approach never dispelled my depression.

In 2019, after taking antidepressants for twelve years, I started to question why some people overcame depression and I couldn't. I began to think surely, if other people could stop being depressed, there was a potential that I could too. How was I different from other people? I pondered this as I hung out the washing in and around my kids playing. Then I claimed the moment to ask for help.

In my lounge room, with my palms together at my heart, I called, 'Bring me the teachers that will help me stop being depressed.' Just weeks later, I was introduced to the Kiloby Inquiries[2] , a set of advanced mindfulness techniques to help me unhook from my negative sense of self, process my emotional pain, trauma and baggage, and overcome mental illness. I began learning these techniques as soon as possible.

The next six months saw me applying these techniques to my daily triggers, and my mental health gradually improved. I couldn't believe it. If only I was shown these techniques when I was fourteen, my life would have looked very differently. While monitored by my doctor, I stopped taking antidepressants and relied on the techniques, my own inner resources and Body Intelligence instead. Within months, I no longer had depression.

Finding a new way to treat my mental illness showed me there was something missing for me all along. Spending twenty years in talk therapy and without improvement had me believe there was something wrong with me. But no one had shown me how to feel safe, to feel my feelings. No one showed me how to befriend my negative thoughts. And certainly, no one showed me that what my body needed from me was love so it could process its own emotions.

The treatment I received from my psychologists and counsellors was talk therapy. I talked through my problems to find solutions. This is a cognitive-based, or mind-based approach. Yet the mind is interlinked with the body and cannot be treated as a separate entity. The mind holds the thoughts, yet the body holds the emotions. Emotions are stored in the body.[3]

While talk therapy encouraged me to *talk* about my feelings, I was never shown how to *feel* my feelings in a safe way. Once I learnt how to feel safe with my pain, I realised this simple practice eased the intensity of both my emotions and thoughts. This somatic, or body-based approach unravelled my nervous system from its state of protection[4] into a place of connection. I felt more comfortable in my own skin and developed more authentic relationships with others.

Fortunately, new evidence on trauma, the brain, and the body shows why talk therapy doesn't work for everyone[5]. A somatic-based approach is the answer for many. Learning how to safely feel your emotions is integral to treating trauma and improving mental health. If you don't relate to the word trauma, we will explore this topic in Chapter Three so you can see if it correlates to you.

Seth Porges, son of Stephen Porges, professor of psychiatry and founder of the ground-breaking polyvagal theory[6] commented on his father's work, 'trauma is not a psychological issue. It's a physiological issue.'[7] In Chapter Three, I will explain neuroscience in simple terms, and why reframing thoughts, staying positive and being resilient doesn't always work for people with mental illness.

Not only did the Kiloby Inquiries help me build a healthy relationship with my emotions, they also showed me what to do with the negative stories in my head. So often in talk therapy, I was encouraged to reframe my negative thoughts to positive ones, but with the endless stream of negativity in my mind this became exhausting and impossible. The Kiloby Inquiries gave me simple and practical steps to take when I am triggered, and when the negative thoughts inevitably arrive.

Talking to someone about painful memories when I was depressed was not as helpful as I find it now that my depression is gone. I no longer fear drowning in bad memories as the Kiloby Inquiries allowed me to feel safe with the difficult memories, which no longer have a harsh impact on me.

While learning simple ways to manage my negative thoughts and reduce the intensity of my emotions was profound, I discovered something greater. We have an incredible intelligence within our bodies that naturally processes our emotions without us *doing* anything except putting our love and attention on our emotions. I call this in-built intelligence, "Body Intelligence". The techniques I will share with you in this book guides you to find your own Body Intelligence.

We are living in a time where we have forgotten fundamental skills to manage our human experience. Whether we suffer from mental illness or not, we all experience intense emotions and negative thoughts through challenging events and circumstances. The act of simply directing our compassionate attention to the feelings in our bodies to manage intense emotions is lost knowledge. It's time to reclaim this ancient wisdom and trust our bodies.

So, if you've been going to talk to someone and you've still got depression, you're not alone. And you're not broken. There is nothing wrong with you. My experience showed me the full spectrum of services that people with depression and anxiety might need, including cognitive-based and somatic-based services, are not always offered. A somatic approach, where you build a healthy relationship with your nervous system and emotions, was the piece I was missing to improve my mental health.

Right now, it's critical that we offer a comprehensive mental health system. In 2019, before the string of pandemic-related lockdowns, 3318 people in Australia suicided.[8] One in five Australians aged 16-85 experience a mental illness in any year.[9] Integrating a somatic approach into treatment for those with depression and anxiety could save lives.

Perhaps you think nothing will work for you, including what I share in this book. Perhaps you feel like you've tried everything. I felt like that too. I suffered with depression for over half of my life and thought I would be on antidepressants for the rest of my days. My mind screamed horrendous stories at me, and I've not wanted to wake up in the mornings. There have been times when I've wanted to check out of life because it was just too hard. I've been a binge-eater, and felt so much shame and disgust being me. I've had dysfunctional relationships and stroked a healthy phone addiction. But I've come out the other side.

I don't have depression anymore. I am no longer weighed down, lost, confused and exhausted. Instead, I have the tools to befriend my thoughts, hold love for my emotions, and take care of my nervous system. Knowing you have the tools to combat the horrible thoughts so you don't fall apart is vital. Imagine if your thoughts could wash off you like water off a duck's back? Stay open to the possibilities.

This book is for you if you've spent months, years, or decades talking to professionals and gotten nowhere. It's for you if deep down, you feel broken, like a failure, bad, or wrong. Or maybe you've accepted you've got depression but you're curious about what you could lift from reading this book. Maybe you look at everyone around you and think, *how do they just get on with life when I am stuck here in this mess with depression and there is no answer for me?* I hear you.

Our journey together might not always feel like sunshine and roses. You're here to do some heavy lifting. You might feel challenged at times and perhaps some negativity will be stirred up. But when you are courageous enough to lift the bonnet to see the junk underneath, nothing will be as bad as you think. And a heads-up, there may be many mic-dropping epiphanies!

My long battle with depression was driven by the fear of feeling the pain, and had me run for years. But when I was shown the gentle and slow way to feel safe in my pain, everything got better. I found the beauty, peace, and freedom within my pain. I healed from the inside out.

You don't need to be terrified venturing into your pain. You get to choose every step you make on your pathway to healing. I will take things very slowly and be by your side. You'll learn the three parts that make up your depression, and the simple steps to dismantle it in those moments it arises – even when it looks like everything around you is falling apart.

Before we start, what is your intention? How would you like to feel as you read this book? How would you like to feel by the end of this book? What do you want to get from this book? Be clear and specific. Take the time to check in with your heart and ask it what it needs and wants. Then trust and thank life for meeting your heart's needs.

If I could give you one tip for our journey together, it would be to complete the practices set out within the book. It's one step to learn the techniques and quite another to put them into regular practise. My depression dissolved through dedicating myself to the techniques. I paid for one-on-one Kiloby Inquiries sessions so I could master the techniques. I planted my bottom on my meditation cushions to practise those techniques, and devoted myself to the practices to see the magic unfold. Change requires commitment. Throughout the chapters, there are explanations of techniques plus QR codes for audio guides and videos to help you practise the techniques. It's not a quick fix but it does work.

You will need a physical space and support around you to complete the practices. Firstly, you will need a place to sit. Preferably, somewhere that is quiet, away from others, and is ready to be used whenever you need. I keep my three cushions on the floor of my bedroom at all times, so I have no excuses but to sit myself down and practise. Secondly, let your loved ones or those you live with know that you are learning something new that is important to you. Tell them you need ten-minute slots without interruption, daily. Explain your why to them. And finally, take this seriously. This book could be the thing that changes your life completely. By the time you've read this book in its entirety, your life could be on a completely new trajectory; one you never thought possible.

CHAPTER ONE
Deep Rest

If you want to be well, the first step is to witness if illness has become identity.
- Dr. Nicole LePera

The first time I started to feel funny, weird, and not my usual self, was weeks after my parents separated. Mum and I had flown back home to Australia after having lived in Thailand with Dad for six months. I was trying to find my feet after having plans upended. We were meant to be in Thailand for three years for Dad's work. I had left my friends, my school, my home and my country to live on what felt like to my then 13-year-old self, a whole new planet. But this monumental move overseas became the end of Mum and Dad's marriage and the breaking apart of my life.

Within weeks of returning to home soil with Mum, and to be reunited with my sisters in Templestowe – back then a slower north-eastern suburb of Melbourne – I remember lying on my floral-draped bed, feeling like the ground had given way beneath me. With Dad now living overseas, Mum absent and suffering an emotional breakdown, what used to be a solid family, was no longer. Nothing felt stable. The once strong and certain walls of my room felt like they could cave in at any moment. Just like my family.

I didn't see Mum and Dad's separation coming. I thought our family was going to be together forever. Suddenly, everything that felt secure had shattered. I felt unsafe, uncertain, unsure. I didn't know who I was or where I belonged. The house bustled with people coming and going. A family friend was living with us at the time, and my sisters were busy with their own young adult lives. I felt voiceless, lonely, confused, and invisible.

My family worried about me. Mum kept assuring me that the separation wasn't my fault. My family would tell me that they were here for me whenever I wanted to talk. And I desperately wanted to talk. But this one voice in my head kept telling me it would be selfish to open up and share with them, while another part of me mentally screamed for them to listen to me. I desperately wanted to be heard and reassured, but I couldn't get the words out. So I remained silent.

All the teachers at school knew what had happened, and I could tell they wanted to help. But no one could make me speak. No one could make everything okay. No one could glue my family back together. I was crumbling inside, pieces of me falling into a deep, dark hole. I tried to make sense of my feelings, but it was like I was walking around in a daze.

I was a mess of confusion, and didn't know how I was meant to act. When the devastating memories of my family falling apart surfaced, they dragged me into wallowing pain. People around me 'there-there-ed' me with concerned looks, but I feared I was an annoying burden. So I pretended to be upbeat and happy. I would swing from pretending to be happy to drowning in my own self-pity. Everyone tip-toed around me, and I couldn't find my equilibrium.

I felt weird. I couldn't understand what was happening to me, although I had a sense there was an extraordinary amount of undealt pain hidden deep within me. And if anyone drew my attention to it, I shut down, too terrified to go there. It was all too much.

Everything was too much. Too hard. I wasn't good enough. I wasn't enough. Life didn't make sense. I didn't know who I was meant to be. So I became the sad and depressed one. There was safety in that role because I knew who I was. I was the one who was sad and depressed. I could *be* that person and know what to do. Look downcast. Don't smile. Don't engage in conversation.

Becoming this sad and depressed person had people come to me. After feeling so lost with our family unit breaking down, I felt comforted when I played the role of the victim. When I was sad and depressed, people would come to ask if I was okay. They came to sit with me. They tried to make me laugh. With them, I wasn't alone. That helped me feel safe in an uncertain and confusing world.

I still didn't say much, though. I didn't know how to voice my feelings. People would say I bottled things up, which ripped me apart. Each time I heard them tell me I had to let my thoughts and feelings out, I automatically heard stories in my head that said: 'you're doing it wrong' and 'you're failing'. I didn't know *how* to let my thoughts and feelings out.

Anything that was said to me, albeit with the best intentions, I took personally. It ripped my insides to shreds, and I metaphorically beat myself up against a brick wall. Life with depression was like drowning in a sea of negativity. I was so sad. And I didn't know how to get myself out of this sad, heavy place.

One of my favourite schoolteachers once said to me, 'Bronte, where's that happy person that you used to be?' Almost like a knee-jerk reaction, the people-pleaser in me transformed my solemn face into a spritely cheer. I put on a shiny mask and pretended to be light and energised. But deep down, I felt very heavy and very sad.

When I told Mum once that I had been crying with a friend at school that day, she said, 'Oh Bronte, people won't want to hang around someone who is sad all the time'. This confused me, but I took it as a rule to abide by: don't be sad.

My family didn't like seeing me sad. Mum would reminisce on how 'happy-go-lucky' I used to be. But I changed. Everything had changed. I was different. It felt like I had this huge, heavy weight around my waist that dragged me down to the ground. I didn't like it, and it appeared others around me didn't like the way I was either. So, I hid this weight and just pretended to be happy.

Pretending to be happy made things worse. I was living a double life. Upbeat and happy on the phone with Nan and Pa, down in the dumps with my immediate family. Toeing the line for some teachers at school, misbehaving with others. I had no idea who I was meant to be for the world, and the positive presentation I portrayed made my inner world worse, darker.

Fast forward a decade, in 2006, the weeks that pulled me into the deepest depression were after I learnt Mum had contracted secondary breast cancer. Three years earlier, she had been stung by her original breast cancer diagnosis at the age of 47; she was just seven years older than her mum (my Nan) had been when *she* was diagnosed with breast cancer. This time, Mum's cancer was in her third-top vertebrae. Finding out Mum's cancer was back, was terrifying.

I was living in Darwin at the time and had just finished my shift at the Boost Juice bar on Mitchell Street when I noticed I had a missed call from my sister. I called her back immediately, excited to hear her voice. As she gently broke the news, the seriousness in her voice made my insides tremble with fear. Carly's question asking me if I was going to fly home made me think, *this is serious*. I remember getting off the phone from Carly and walking blindly across the road, seeing nothing through my hysterical tears. I couldn't contain my heaving sobs as I wove through the passing people. The harrowing thought that Mum was going to die transformed in a flash to a crippling future. *How am I going to survive without her?*

Mum had always been the one who caught me. I was the baby of the family, the youngest of three girls and she was always the one I would turn to when I was lost in my head with nowhere to turn. She would listen to me for hours as I tried to make sense of myself and my crumbling world. She was my biggest cheerleader, encouraging me with words like, 'You can do it.' She let me get what I needed to get off my chest. On my worst days, Mum listened to me cry and cry and cry and cry.

Once I'd flown home back to Melbourne to see Mum, I found a place to live in North Melbourne. I told myself it was time to get myself together. Mum was going to die, and I needed to be able to live without her. I decided I couldn't cry anymore. Crying meant I was failing at life and falling apart. And if I fell apart when Mum was gone, I would die. I thought, *I just need to be stronger and get on with life like everybody else.*

At the time, I was working as a Casual Relief Teacher in primary schools all around Melbourne. But every day, I needed to cry. I would wake up with overwhelming waves of tears rising up my throat. But I swallowed them back. Crying was no longer an option for me. If I wanted to survive without Mum, I had to take control and stop crying.

In my full-length mirror, dressed ready to teach for the day, I would look at myself through eyes filled with tears. With self-hatred, I would forcefully push my tears away and tell myself not to cry.

One day, I managed to keep my tears behind the floodgates while the designated staff member at the school where I was currently working, showed me to my classroom. Then once I was alone in the classroom, I burst into tears. My body felt like a broken dam, and I feared these tears just would not stop. What was wrong with me? I would think with disgust.

When I interacted with people at school, I pretended to be enthusiastic and full of energy. By the end of the day, I would fall in an exhausted heap from hiding my inner turmoil, from attempting to keep my crying at bay. I never had any energy to cook myself anything worth eating. So I binged on chocolate, Twisties, and fried food. Whenever I wanted Mum to save me, I refrained from calling because she was sick. I needed to fix myself on my own. I thought I just needed to try harder.

In a time that felt like I couldn't carry it all on my own anymore, I timidly spilled my despair with my sister Carly. I told her I needed to cry every day, and she told me there was support available for that. I had always been resistant when Mum had ever suggested I go on antidepressants. Being on antidepressants meant I had failed in life. It was like trying really hard on all of my exams at life-school then being given the 'nope, you couldn't do it' report card from the world.

But that day Carly framed medication in a new way for me. She told me it was resourceful of me. Like I was taking good care of myself and taking personal responsibility. I walked away from that conversation with her with hope for a more positive future and with a possibility that there was a way out of my tumultuous, painful life.

At the age of 23, after nine years of undiagnosed depression I finally surrendered, was clinically diagnosed with depression and started taking antidepressants. I had mixed emotions about it all – failure, relief, and hope. Despite feeling like I had failed, having my GP explain mental illness as a chemical imbalance in the brain brought immense relief. If there was a chemical imbalance in my brain, then that meant it was out of my control, that it wasn't my fault. I *hadn't* failed. Maybe depression was hereditary, not because I couldn't get myself together. A sense of pressure alleviated upon hearing my depression may not have been something I brought on myself.

Having a name for what I had been feeling helped me make sense of it. I started calling it 'my depression', and it felt like it became a part of me. Rather than trying to be normal like everyone else, it was a relief knowing I didn't have to fight the depression anymore – I could just be depressed. And that was okay.

Having depression and being on antidepressants became a part of who I was. Depression became part of my identity and my make-up. It was a part of me that felt solid and certain. Taking antidepressants solidified my relationship with my illness. I was used to listing Escitalopram on my medical forms and figured I would do that for the rest of my life. Depression was a label I had hung over my head.

When I was coming to terms with taking antidepressants, I treated my depression like a broken leg – if you break your leg, you put it in plaster. If you have depression, you take medication to fix it. This helped keep at bay the intensity of the stories in my head that said I was weak.

After the initial weeks on medication, feeling spacey and like I was here but not here, I started to adapt to antidepressants. Life began to feel easier, and I felt normal. I didn't wake up in the mornings disappointed that I was alive. My body wasn't plagued with lethargy, and it felt easier to get out of bed. I got my life back. I could socialise without drowning in my own self-misery and I could put a load of washing on effortlessly.

Medication helped me finish my degrees and start my career as a teacher. I travelled the world with my now husband, Leigh, and we planted our roots in the town I always wanted to live in – Bendigo. We grew the most beautiful family of three children: Jackson, Ivy, and Maggie. And I built a business for which my creative spirit yearned.

Every now and then, when life got stressful, my depression re-entered my world. It felt like a big black shadow lurking in the background that would start to creep over my shoulder and taunt me. It was present enough for me to know it was always there. On more difficult days, it would linger and threaten to stay. I was terrified this feeling would keep returning and stay longer each time. My worst nightmare was that it would wrap its black fingers around me, pull me into its eternal darkness and have me disappear forever.

Despite the benefits I received from taking medication, most of the time I didn't want to take it. When I took medication, I felt fine, like I didn't have a mental illness. Often, I would think that I was taking medication for no reason. Many times, I tried to come off my medication. I would forget how bad my depression could get and thought I could manage life without the antidepressants. Up until 2019, I had no success.

Every time I came off the medication, that horrible lurking feeling would return. The thought of it overwhelming me was enough to go back on them with a great sense of shame. I was annoyed that I couldn't face life head-on like others. After my failed attempts, I would hear surrounding loved ones say, 'some people just have to be on them for the rest of their lives.' I had put myself in that category; that I had depression and that was that. I mentally accepted that I would have depression for the rest of my life.

The Roots

The truth is, the building blocks of my depression began well before Mum and Dad separated. I was unconsciously forming a web of stories about myself that left me feeling like a bad girl, not good enough, and like there was something wrong with me.

As a student at my new school in Grade 2, I remember being called a 'freckle face'. As a stickler for rules, I went straight to the teacher to tell her. When I told her, she gave me the impression I wasn't meant to come to her for situations like this, and that I needed to try and work this problem out myself. I was confused. I thought I had done the right thing. A sensitive soul, I thought I was doing things wrong.

When I was a kid, I was always told I was too sensitive. In Grade 4, I warmed to the music teacher. She was cheeky and I liked her. One afternoon, Mrs Smith visited our classroom and amongst the crowd of kids sitting on the floor with our classroom teacher, Mrs Smith made a light-hearted joke with me. She had a way about her that had me feel special because she made little jokes between her and I. I felt included and loved by her. She gave me a twinkle in her eye and a tiny smirk at the corner of her mouth that told me we were having fun together. Interjecting, my classroom teacher stole the fun and laughed condescendingly about me to Mrs Smith saying, 'Ohh, don't say that, she'll cry.' At that moment, a part of me broke. I instantly felt 'weak, too precious and too sensitive'.

As the baby of the family, I often cried, particularly when saying goodbye to my best friend. Kindred spirits, she had moved away and we only saw each other on school holidays. I would cry before I saw her, I cried while we caught up playing together, and I cried when we parted. Everyone around me looked perplexed that I cried so much. I thought it was weird that I was crying yet the more I tried to stop crying, the more I needed to cry.

It wasn't only personal relationships that had me feel so much, but also my relationship with the world. For as long as I can remember I have felt I was here on the planet for a reason to help in an important way. I always had a knowing I was here to change the world for the better. A big purpose like this can be overwhelming for a sensitive soul who feels things deeply. I had an immense sense of dread being alive because the weight of fixing the world felt too much.

On challenging days, the world looked like it was doing more harm than good, and the immensity of change that was required was damning. At my lowest of low points, I hadn't wanted to be here.

In my exhaustion, I felt like there was no point in life. Making the simplest decisions had felt insurmountable. I'd been so tired just from walking a very short distance. All of this culminated under an umbrella labelled: depression.

When I was twenty, home from University, I still remember sitting in Mum's brown leather armchair in the dimly-lit lounge room, crying. I was overwhelmed by the state of the world, trying to work out how I was going to fix all its problems. I was worried about the devastation of the environment, distraught about children in Africa I saw on World Vision ads who were malnourished and dying. It all felt like too much. I didn't know which way to go first, which action to take, and I wondered how I was going to save everyone and everything. It was a very heavy load and immense pressure for a young woman to have on her shoulders.

Do you feel like this? Like you're here to bring positive change to the planet? Have you exhausted yourself or felt depleted or overwhelmed trying to fix, save and heal the world? Maybe you've felt like it's not okay to cry, that you're too sensitive or doing life 'wrong'. You're in good company. And perhaps the stories you hear in your mind are different to mine. All are welcome. The concepts and techniques I will show you in this book can be used on any problem you have in your life and help you realise that you are none of the negative stories in your head.

For me, it was at the beginning of 2019 when I started questioning when the time would come for me to conquer my depression, to leave it all behind. Around that time, I had an influx of clients who were experiencing mental illness; they all wanted to be able to manage their depression and anxiety without medication. My clients' needs often reflect my own and even though my antidepressants had helped me through, I could relate to their desire to be medication-free.

At the time, I was planning a retreat with a cacao ceremony, which is a ceremonial drink to open your heart, connect to the Earth and listen to your wisdom within. Drinking ceremonial cacao can have contra-indications with those who take antidepressants. I was excited about participating in a cacao ceremony and I didn't like the thought of me missing out on one of the best workshops at my own retreat.

This had me decide it was time. I was going to do the work on myself with KI (the Kiloby Inquiries) to come off antidepressants and attend the cacao ceremony. The ceremony was in October, so I had a date to be medication-free. It was like a line in the sand. And boy, was I terrified! But I was excited too. And curious to know if I could shake my depression for good.

Three Things

Now I am going to introduce you to the first concept in the Kiloby Inquiries that changed the way I saw my depression, myself and the world. When I learnt this simple information, I had one big penny drop. Please take notes. You don't want to miss this. Are you ready?

All meaning we create is made of three things: words, pictures, and body sensations. Everything in life can be narrowed down to these three things. The words are the stories, thoughts and dialogue we hear in our heads. The pictures are mental imagery; they could be memories of the past, potential projections of what might happen in the future or even a made-up scenario of what might be happening right now. We see these pictures through the mind. The body sensations are the sensations we feel such as heat in our face, tingling in the arms, hard pressure on the chest, a tightening of the belly or pain in the head or neck. This is by no means an exhaustive list. When the words and pictures present simultaneously with body sensations, our sense of reality is strong, and we make meaning from our life. It feels real. It feels like it's really happening *right now*.

Let's imagine you've been trying to avoid a certain person in your life because you made a fool of yourself in front of them recently, then you see them at the shops. You might have the words '*Oh no*' come into your mind when you see them. Let's imagine that you try to avoid eye contact so you don't have to speak to that person, but they see you and are heading your way. As they are walking towards you, you might have an image in your mind of you saying something stupid or making an idiot out of yourself in front of them again. And you might feel a lump or contraction in your throat. In this scenario the words are 'oh no', the picture or image is of you being an idiot, and the sensation is a tight throat.

The most fundamental concept in the Kiloby Inquiries is the Velcro Effect. When I learnt this, the pain that I struggled with began to heal. Keep reading as I explain, or watch me explain via video when you scan this QR code:

We all know what Velcro is; that stuff that has two parts that stick together. In the case of the Velcro Effect, the top layer of Velcro is the words and pictures (these come from the mind) and the bottom layer of the Velcro is the sensations in the body. The body and mind work together for so many of our daily functions, and when we make meaning, this is no different. When the words and pictures are stuck to the sensations in the body, that's when we are stuck in our story, stuck in the meaning we've made about the situation, stuck in the mess, triggered, in discomfort and pain. We are 'stuck in Velcro'.

For every problem we have in our life, there are either words, pictures, or both with body sensations. Let's look at some examples. You might feel like life is too hard to deal with. These are the words. 'Life is too hard to deal with'. That thought might come with images of all of the things you have to get done like bills to pay, clothes to buy, people to contact and emails to reply to. And with 'life is too hard to deal with' and the mental imagery of all the things that need doing, maybe there's a contraction in your belly, heat in your cheeks or a heaviness on your shoulders.

Let's look at another example. Maybe you're trying to reach a goal and you're getting frustrated and angry that the goal hasn't yet been achieved. You might hear the words 'I can't do it' in your head. Perhaps a picture of someone you admire and at times feel envious or even jealous of who has already achieved the goal you're striving for flashes through your mind. And coupled with the words 'I can't do it', and the picture of the person you're envious of, comes the sensation that could be a tightening of the throat, a hardening in the jaw or a shooting sensation up the legs. Every single problem in our lives is simply made of words, pictures, and body sensations.

You might be well aware of having mental words or even pictures of people or situations in your mind but can't relate to the type of sensations that I'm describing. If that's you, you're not alone. Most of us live our lives in our heads, completely disconnected from what's happening in the body. This is called 'dissociation'[10] and can happen as a result of exhausting the fight or flight response from distressing or traumatic experiences in our lives. So much so that we end up 'freezing', collapsing, disconnecting and zoning out from our bodies as a way of coping. I certainly had no idea what was happening in my body. Finding a yoga teacher who fosters interoceptive awareness is a great first step to increasing connection with your body's sensations.

The truth is that the body and mind are inherently linked.[11] Try imagining that you have a big juicy lemon in your hand, and you bite down hard on it. What happened? Did you start producing more saliva in your mouth? Not only does the body play an integral role in our capacity to be alive, our connection to and relationship with our bodies is essential for improved mental health.

One challenging moment of my day parenting three young children is waiting for my kids to go to the toilet and go to bed. By the end of the day, I am done. I'm tired. Exhausted in fact. I can feel the time and space I will have on my own in just a couple of minutes and my kids are taking forever to go to the toilet and climb into bed. I'm looking at my middle child who is laughing and dancing and having the most magical time playing in her room instead of going to bed. And my eldest is taking his sweet little time to do his wee, flush the toilet, wash his hands, dry his hands, turn the lights off and shut the doors. I. Just. Want. Them. In. Bed. So often, I have felt ready to explode.

At this moment, I'm stuck in Velcro. The words 'GET IN BED NOW' are Velcro-ed to the rising pressure through my chest, throat and cheeks. On my worst days I raise my voice and project my frustration onto them as if they are the problem. If they got in bed everything would be fine. What is more accurate to say is that if they were in bed, this explosive sensation in my body would dissipate. It's the body sensation that is what makes the experience difficult.

In the coming chapters I am going to show you how to dismantle yourself from the Velcro Effect so this explosive sense of impatience and frustration you might feel with your loved ones can be processed as they arise in the moment.

What situations do you have in your life where you are stuck in Velcro? In your hot mess? Angry? Frustrated? Sad? Depressed? Lonely? Exhausted? Jealous? Grab your journal and pick one problem you're dealing with. List the mental dialogue you hear in your head when you are thinking about that problem. The thoughts you write down are the words. Notice the pictures that pop up in your head. Are they pictures of people or specific scenarios that have happened? Are they projected conversations or situations that might happen in the future? These are the pictures. The words and pictures make up the top layer of Velcro. And finally, what is the body doing? Take a moment to think about the problem. Then take a breath and focus your attention on the body. Is there a pain in your chest? A slight tingling in your arms? Or is it something else? It might feel strange to feel the sensations in your body at first but stay with it. The body is the key to dissolving your depression.

I always just thought it was my mind that was the problem. I just wanted my mind to stop making such horrific stories about myself so I could get on with life and be the amazing person I knew I could be. I didn't realise that for every time something went wrong in my life, or I was moody, low or depressed, there was a whole lot of sensations going on in my body. I dismissed my emotions as a waste of time, not worthy of engagement. I hadn't spent time in my body. In fact, I'd often heard people say, 'go to the body' or 'stay in the body', and dismissed it with 'what does that even mean?'. Then I'd focus my attention on trying to change my mindset. I didn't get it.

Not only did the Velcro Effect open a doorway to understanding my depression, there was a beautiful relief that it was okay to have these words in my mind. That there was nothing wrong with me for having these stories in my head. For the first time, no one was trying to change my thinking or change my mind. I always thought that was my problem; that I had all of these bad thoughts in my head and I needed to stop them somehow but couldn't. Just having someone break down a problem of mine into three simple and tangible parts – words, pictures and body sensations – brought a feeling of acknowledgement for the stories in my head. For so long, yet out of their sheer love for me, I'd been given positive pep talks from others which left me feeling more inadequate. The Velcro Effect validated all the mental stories I'd heard and invited me in to explore my body's responses to specific challenges and triggers.

Learning the Velcro Effect was simple. I could get my head around it. This wasn't rocket-science, I didn't feel like an idiot, and it made total sense! I was spurred on to learn more. Knowing the Velcro Effect was the start of something profound.

Being aware that there are words, pictures and body sensations can give you some insight about yourself from day-to-day and it can build your self-awareness. The next step is to know how to remove the top layer from the bottom layer, so you're not stuck in Velcro, stuck in your story, stuck in the mess.

Stay with me.

CHAPTER TWO
Deficiency

It's not what happened in childhood that's the problem. It's what we made it mean for ourselves that is the problem. And what we carry about it in ourselves.
- **Gabor Maté**

When I began practising the Kiloby Inquiries, I became acutely aware of all the negative beliefs or stories I held about myself. I didn't consciously choose these beliefs or stories; they were created automatically in my mind. I will refer to these beliefs and stories as 'deficiency stories' and 'core deficiency stories'. Deficiency stories and core deficiency stories are the negative beliefs we have about ourselves, about who we are and how we fit into the world. This collection or web of stories creates our negative sense of self or deficient self.

Examples of my own deficiency stories have been: 'I'm a loser', 'I'm an idiot', 'I'm hopeless', 'I'm a nutcase', 'I'm stupid', 'I'm dumb', 'I'm wrong'. The more depressed I became, the more I identified with these stories as if they were true. As my mental health improved, the less I identified with these stories and saw them for all that they were; words.

Core deficiency stories are the root of deficiency stories. They are the root beliefs or stories we have about ourselves that tell us we are deficient in some way. Examples of *core* deficiency stories are: 'I'm unlovable', 'I'm not worthy', 'I'm not enough', 'I'm not safe', 'I'm alone', 'I'm unwanted'.

It's not your fault if you have negative stories about yourself. You're not failing if you have a negative sense of self. Everyone hears negative stories about themselves in their heads, even if they are fleeting from time to time. It's an inevitable part of the human experience. And when you have the right tools, you don't have to be stuck with them forever.

It is helpful to identify the stories so you can apply techniques to them and process them. This has them dissolve, has you unhook from them so you don't identify with those stories and believe they are true. The techniques also help you feel safe when these stories arise, and short-circuits the looping cycle of spiralling into depression.

These are what I would call 'painful stories' we have about ourselves. They are the stories that hurt to even speak them or be reminded of them. These are the stories we hear being screamed at us on difficult days. They are the stories we try to block out, avoid, ignore, keep away and push down. And they are the root of all our suffering. While I had been shown how to reframe my beliefs to more positive language, I never had anyone show me how to let go of these negative stories like the Kiloby Inquiries did, in the most gentle, loving, simple and profoundly life changing way.

Our deficiency stories and core deficiency stories drive all the problems on the everyday, surface-level of our lives. I like to use a tree as a metaphor when describing how our problems, deficiency stories and core deficiency stories work together. The roots of the tree symbolise the core deficiency stories. The tree grows from the roots and creates a solid foundation through the trunk, which represents our own set (or web) of beliefs, sense of identity, or idea of who we are. From the trunk grow branches; these branches are limbs that stem from the roots – they are the deficiency stories that are driven by the core deficiency stories. The leaves are the surface-level problems we see in our everyday lives that are primarily driven by our core deficiency stories and deficiency stories. Have a look at the diagram to get super clear on this.

This web of interconnectedness that tells us who we are, shows us how we keep attracting the same problems in our lives over and over again. Maybe you keep finding yourself in relationships that leave you feeling awful. Your core deficiency story could be 'I'm not enough' or 'I'm not worthy'. Perhaps whenever you join a new club or meet a new group of friends, you never feel like you belong. Your core deficiency story could be 'I don't belong'. You might always have money troubles and stress to scrape enough together to make ends meet. In this case, a core deficiency story of yours could be 'I'm unsafe'. When we are hooked to our subconscious or unconscious stories, this creates our reality and shapes our lives. Taking the time to address these stories using a somatic-based approach has you relax and realise deep down that you are none of them.

Generally speaking, you might have between a handful of core deficiency stories and many more deficiency stories. If you're getting stuck on trying to work out your deficiency stories, trust that they will become clear as we continue to spend time together. Deficiency stories and core deficiency stories tend to start with 'I', 'I am' or 'I am not'. Remember, they are telling you how you are deficient in some way. Together, your core deficiency stories and deficiency stories make up the web of stories that tell you, you are deficient or lacking in some way. If you're overwhelmed with the amount of deficiency stories you have, that's common too. You're not broken if you have a lot of deficiency stories.

I remember being in the car with Mum and my sisters when I would have been as young as five years old. Mum was cross with me and told me that I had been a naughty girl over the past few weeks. As a child, those words jarred me, and from that moment I remember seeing myself through a new lens. I felt like I was inherently bad. I felt rejected, different from my sisters, outcast, separated from my family and alone. I no longer belonged, and I thought there was something wrong with me. I told myself I needed to try better to be better, so I was accepted, loved and embraced.

Memories like these are not a poor reflection of Mum; she loved me with all her heart. She wasn't trying to hurt me. As a mother myself, I know how difficult it can be to create positive boundaries for my children while managing my own fatigue and frustration. We all do the best that we can, in the situation we are in, with the resources we have at each moment. Mum is not to blame for the meaning that I made from this experience; it just happened automatically.

I'm sure my stories are conjuring up those significant moments in your life where your deficiency stories formed, and you automatically started to see yourself through a negative lens. Sometimes we can remember these moments while others are buried deep within our unconscious. In Chapter Three, I will show you how to identify your deficiency stories from any memory you've had using a technique called the Boomerang. And then you will learn what to do with the Boomerang so you don't have to keep carrying the stories around with you.

When you start to identify the deficiency stories in you, you realise they play out in various areas of your life. The dissatisfaction I felt in my family relationships were just as prevalent in my friendships. I felt invisible, that no one 'got' me and understood how hard things were.

In my late teens, I vividly remember crying in the car after going out for breakfast with a close friend. There was this overwhelming sense that she didn't see me, that I didn't receive the support I wanted from her. I remember thinking that she spent the whole time talking about herself and didn't ask me once how I was. This story – they're not asking about me – was driven by the deficiency story, 'no one cares about me', 'I don't matter', and 'I'm worthless'. Core deficiency stories drive all problems in life.

Identifying our core deficiency stories is essential but not enough on its own. I remember in the various psychologist rooms I found myself in, we would arrive at realising what the professionals would call my 'core beliefs' and while I felt a greater sense of understanding about myself and why I tick the way I do, I never knew what to do with the core belief once I became aware of it. I got stuck in the spiralling misery of the core belief and didn't know how to let it go.

Knowing our core beliefs is just the start. Chapter Five will show you how you can dissolve the core belief so it doesn't keep dictating your life the way it always has, and you start breaking the cycle of attracting the same thing over and over in your life.

From an early age we naturally form a sense of identity. We are tall or short, have brown hair or blue eyes, we have favourite colours, footy teams, animals. We learn we are good at some subjects and not at others. We develop a sense of who we are. As we go through life, we have significant experiences that shape how we see ourselves and we inherently create both a positive and negative sense of self.

If you are like me, you have spent much of your life running from your negative sense of self and mental construct of deficiency.

We try to be something good in life in the fear that we are bad, and spend our lives acting and behaving in ways to counteract our feelings of inadequacy that are buried deep within us. What if we, as a collective human race, began to look at our own negative self-beliefs rather than run from them? If we did, we would all realise we weren't any of these stories. We would be clear, light, peaceful, and free human beings interacting and engaging with each other and the world in a very different way.

Practise natural rest

The first step to end the struggle with living with the stories in your mind is to return to natural rest. Your resting state. You might know it as mindfulness. Being aware of what is present rather than being stuck in your head. When you're aware of what's happening in the body, you can hear sounds and you can feel the touch of air on your face. This is when the ventral vagal branch of the parasympathetic nervous system is activated in the body, rather than the fight or flight response in the sympathetic nervous system.[12] This is when you feel safe. This is when your primal self is not preparing your body to run from or fight a threat. This is when you are relaxed in your mind and free to feel your body. *This* is your natural state.

In reality though, our lives look like a constant state of stress. We feel like we need a year-long holiday to catch up on sleep, relaxation, and rest. We're so deprived of rest that the idea of it feels unattainable. Many of us these days find ourselves in a subtle or not-so-subtle state of stress response every day, and the idea of returning the body and mind to a resting state seems impossible. We are triggered left, right and centre every day, and live in a perpetual state of survival, or go-go-go.

The idea of viewing the resting state as our normal state of being might sound strange or unachievable. Rest and relaxation is something we might squeeze into our annual holiday if we're lucky, in between being busy sightseeing and ticking off the list of must-do attractions. For most of us, we spend our waking days running from one thing to another to keep up with everyday life. Work, school permission slips, dinner dates, kids' parties, shopping, swimming lessons, the household, looking after family members, keeping up with the finances, checking on friends... the list is mind-boggling. Some of us even find it hard to sleep at night, let alone rest. We're so exhausted we find ourselves staring at our devices in bed or glued to the couch, scrolling and scrolling, avoiding rest like the plague.

Mindfulness has become very popular in the last twenty years and has brought benefits to many people's lives. But for some, mindfulness sounds like this elusive thing that leaves people confused. That's why I prefer the term 'natural rest'. Natural rest means that you are resting, naturally. Resting with everything that is here at this moment. The space in the room, the book or device you're holding, your body, your breath, the smells, sensations in the body, the sounds, the words or your thoughts, the mental imagery. *You* are simply resting, watching and noticing what is here... now. Believe it or not, natural rest is our natural state of being.

Natural rest (or mindfulness) has swept the world, through schools, hospitals, homes and workplaces. This ancient practice has helped us feel a sense of calm and peace as we navigate living in a crazily accelerated and fast-paced world. Mindfulness is an integral first step to regulate the nervous system, return the body and mind to homeostasis and experience a sense of calm.

Mindfulness is abundantly supported by science, showing many benefits including:

- reduced stress, anxiety and depressive symptoms
- increased resilience and peace of mind
- strengthening of the prefrontal cortex and hippocampus (key brain areas for learning and wellbeing)
- enhanced cognitive performance, e.g. concentration, memory and processing speed boosts to study and work performance
- improved creativity, mental flexibility and problem-solving ability
- enhanced communication and leadership
- improved relationships (with your partner, family, colleagues and friends). [13]

I was sixteen when I began practising mindfulness, meditation and breathing practices. After my parents separated, and life at home was hard, I would hide behind my closed doors to follow the breathing tips in the Health and Wellbeing section of my *Dolly* magazines. I used these practices as a way to cope and feel calm in my confusing new life. I went on to practise meditation on and off over the next twenty years. I even dedicated myself to a ten-day Vipassana meditation retreat where I meditated for eleven hours a day! But two years later, I started taking antidepressants.

While meditation gave me short-term relief, it never removed my depression. Similarly to trying to stay positive, trying to stay calm became exhausting too. It felt like I was putting out spot fires every time I was triggered. Everywhere. Every day. I was trying to keep on top of the internal storm that lurked within the depths of me. It was like refusing to look at my messy bedroom. Shutting the doors on the smell in the kitchen cupboard. And then not being able to escape the mess or stench as it wafted and spread throughout my whole house. The more I resisted, the more it persisted. The more it persisted, the more terrified I was of what I would find if I ever looked.

The common problem with mindfulness is that there seems to be no time to add another thing to your self-care list. Our lives are already filled to the brim that we don't have space to add anything more. We want to do so many things and we want to do them all now, that our lives become one big explosion that leaves ourselves running on a treadmill and utterly exhausted. We get so tired that silencing the world with Netflix is normal just to get through each week.

What if rest could come into your life as you were doing things? What if natural rest felt different and even more desirable than flopping on the couch with your phone complaining about how draining and heavy life feels? What if you could rest through every waking part of your day and feel like you were on holiday every day, no matter what you were doing or who you were talking to?

Resting to you might look like laying on the couch checking your phone, but is your mind resting here? Your body might be resting but your mind is probably actively planning, getting back to people or checking notifications. Natural rest involves your body and mind at rest, naturally.

Having all parts of you resting requires you to be aware of what's happening in each moment. You can do it as you read this. Can you look at the space in the room you're in? Is there space that surrounds your body? Start to notice sensations you can feel in your body. And can you notice there's space in your body where there are no sensations? Can you hear sounds? And can you hear the sound of silence *between* the sounds?

Put more attention on the sensation in your body. Is there tension? Pain? Discomfort? A funny feeling? Often, without being aware of it, we try to escape any discomfort. Discomfort is judged as a problem that needs to be fixed. A lot of the time, we can't let our bodies be just as they are. In this resistance to ourselves, we have lost the deep intrinsic intelligence of the body that looks after the body sensations that feel uncomfortable.

It's radical for us to rest with these sensations as *they* are without trying to fix them, get rid of them or heal them. Often, we are holding onto life with white knuckles obsessively striving to get somewhere in life. So we are somebody. So we have achieved something. Yet allowing ourselves the space to be *in* life just as we are without trying to fix ourselves, change ourselves or make ourselves better, brings radical peace. Driven by deficiency, we don't think it's good or safe enough to let ourselves be just as we are. Allowing tension to be in the body without trying to get rid of it is a radical step towards feeling safe, comfortable, and free in your own skin.

Start to see if you can allow the tension to be in your body without trying to get rid of it. Allow your body to be just as it is with tension or discomfort. Notice there is space around the discomfort and see if you can hold your attention on both the space and the discomfort at the same time. If there's no discomfort in your body, play with a different sensation that is available to you now as you read this.

The first time my KI Facilitator guided me to allow the tension to be in my body, I felt a deep sense of relief. *What do you mean?* I thought. As an intuitive guide, I trained to clear and release blocks or 'negative' energies from my clients' bodies. The simple act of giving myself permission to be exactly as I was without any need to fix me was truly liberating.

Now, notice how your body can rest while you're seated. Whether you're sitting on a chair or on some cushions on the floor, notice how your skeletal system holds you. You have a beautiful stacking of vertebrae that hold you up from your hip bones so you don't even need to try to prop yourself up. The body does it for you. Then you can just let your shoulders hang. Let your arms and hands drop. Have your legs and feet get as heavy as they want to be.

Often, we are desperately trying to keep ourselves 'up' that we've lost our ability to come down and be held by the ever-present stability and support of the ground. Let yourself come to the ground. See how heavy you can make your body. Let your jaw drop to the ground. Have your knees and hips come to the ground. Let gravity take your whole body to the ground. And in this heaviness, start to be curious and notice how it feels to have the body rest.

When you can bring curiosity to how your body feels as it sits there on its own, a space or gap can form where you are *not* your body and this solid sense of self-identity. Instead, there is a quiet part of you that is aware. Like a curious eye watching what is unfolding in each moment. The sensations are simply sensations, and less about who you are. Natural rest is the gateway to your negative sense of self unravelling before your eyes as you simply watch the coming and going of sensations in and around the space inside and outside your body. Practise natural rest with me when you scan this QR code:

Practice Natural Rest:

- feel the sensations in your body
- look for the space inside your body where there are no sensations
- notice how your skeletal system holds your body on its own. You can relax and let the skeletal system hold you up on its own
- let your shoulders, arms, legs, jaw and whole body become heavy... and then heavier
- create space between your top and bottom teeth
- notice how the space between each vertebrae in your spine naturally lengthens and extends your body, effortlessly
- put your attention on the space in front of your body, behind your body, to the left of your body, to the right of your body, above your body and under your body
- listen to the sounds around you as if you've never heard them before
- notice how silence sounds *between* the sounds you can hear
- feel where you can feel your breath moving your body
- watch which parts of your body make contact with the furniture or floor
- notice how it feels to have clothing draped over your body
- notice how it feels to have the vibration of sounds touch your ears

When you practise natural rest, your mind will wander; that's a given. Welcome the wandering too. Allow the distractions, and then once you've realised you've lost your focus, return your attention to your point of focus. This is the process of natural rest. Falling in and out of presence and natural rest. This is welcome because you're human. You're not a robot, you are human. So *let* yourself be human. Natural rest or mindfulness didn't dissolve my depression. But it was a fundamental start. The more you practise this process of resting, the more prepared you will be to process and clear the bigger stuff that's been weighing you down.

CHAPTER THREE
Triggers and Trauma

Trauma is something that happens initially to our bodies and our instincts. Only then do its effects spread to our minds, emotions, and spirits.
- **Peter Levine**

We all know what it's like to be triggered. It might be someone who says something that really gets under your skin. Maybe a pandemic hits, and you're annoyed your beautiful plans have gone out the window. Or it could be a colleague at work you can't stand being around. Or maybe it's a parent who says that thing that makes you want to hang up on them. A trigger is an experience we have that shifts us out of safety and connection and into a level of insecurity and protection.

A trigger is an event, scenario, moment, thought, or idea that activates a mental and/or emotional response in the body. A mental response can be heard in the 'mind dialogue'. Emotions include physical sensations such as a tightness around the throat, a burning sensation in your cheeks, or a pain in your chest. When we're triggered, the mind's words and pictures are stuck to the body's sensations and the Velcro Effect is taking place.

The external stimuli – or things that trigger you – can be subtle in your everyday life. It might be someone smirking at you after you've shared something vulnerable, a support figure saying no when you've asked for help, or a loved one not looking at you when you're craving connection.

These experiences might have you clenching your teeth, biting your lips, spitting hateful remarks, having your heart pumping, or responding in a variety of other ways. But the experience of being triggered is an inescapable part of life. Up until I found the Kiloby Inquiries, I didn't know how to process these intense emotional explosions so skilfully. Often, we are told to suck it up, find a solution and 'get on with it'.

When we start to stop and listen, we realise we are triggered throughout our lives every day. Some triggers are small and subtle, while others are wild and intense. On those wilder days, someone might say a few words of well-meaning advice such as: 'You just need to stay positive', which makes you want to contort into a ball of shame and have the ground swallow you up; or it might crawl at your skin or make you want to throw objects at them with rage.

Sometimes you might not even know you are being triggered. Take waiting as an example. If we are waiting for a page to load on our computer, we might fill that gap of five seconds by checking our phone notifications. If you didn't fill that time and simply waited for the page to load, you might hear yourself whining, '*Come onnnn!*'. This is a trigger too. Your sympathetic nervous system becomes activated. You're gradually shifting out of the resting state that the ventral vagal parasympathetic response offers and moving into a subtle stress response.

Often, we can fall into the illusion that the people in our lives are the cause of our triggers. We blame them. It's their fault. They shouldn't be saying this or doing that.

It's our own judgment of how we think they should behave and relate in the world. 'She triggers the hell out of me' or 'he's doing my head in', I would find myself saying. But when we stop and examine where the trigger is actually occurring, it's happening within ourselves. The words, pictures and body sensations that erupt are within you. And the words, pictures and body sensations are what makes up the trigger. Sure, we might have people in our lives who go out of their way to upset us, and we always have a choice whether to have them in our lives. But ultimately, the trigger has nothing to do with them. The trigger is happening within us.

Often, the person triggering you is just being themselves. They are just going about their day, doing their thing. More likely than not, they're not going out of their way to try to trigger you. They are likely unconsciously relating from their own deficiency stories. They are mixed up in their own words, pictures and body sensations. I'd wager they are doing the best they can from the perception they have of themselves and the world.

Telling ourselves to stop being so judgmental about others can add fuel to our own self-loathing. Knowing how not to take things personally is very difficult when you're stuck in your own hot mess. It hurts when we're triggered. There's emotional pain. It's not a fun feeling. Being laughed at is crushing. Being rejected when you've asked for help can feel soul destroying, hitting you right in the guts. When you're not locking eyes with your loved one when you need that confirmation that you're connected, you can feel alone, lost, confused and abandoned.

The first step to know how to handle a trigger is to know from where it's stemming. Experiences that trigger an intensely negative emotional charge, whether it lasts for a split second or you can feel it for weeks, underneath the surface these experiences are activating or resurfacing your deficiency and core deficiency stories. Your interpretation of the experience is bringing your sense of deficiency to the surface to be seen, heard and felt.

This understanding can help us see that the people who trigger us the most are our best teachers. The person, or scenario with that person, is activating the original deficiency story, and these experiences can confirm our false sense of identity and our core deficiency stories. Once I show you the skills to manage your triggers, you start seeing through your self-identity, and the negative beliefs start to fall away and you find yourself responding to people and situations with a lot less intensity, and a lot more peace.

Triggering experiences differ for everyone. What one person might not think is a triggering experience, might leave another dying inside. When I shared my sadness and depression with Mum, she would often say: "What are we going to do with you?" Like any loving mother watching her daughter in pain, Mum was desperate to see me get better. But *my* interpretation to her rhetorical question was, 'I'm hopeless. I'm a nutcase. Nothing will fix me. There's something wrong with me.'

This deficiency story – 'there's something wrong with me' – can be more clearly refined to: 'I'm wrong', which has played out in many situations throughout my life. I developed habits of always needing to be right, to prove myself and everyone else around me that I wasn't wrong.

I never knew what to do when I was triggered. Often, I would just ruminate and replay the scenario over and over, those hurtful words playing on repeat. It was obnoxiously loud and I couldn't shut it off. Sometimes binge eating helped.

In KI, we use a technique to find out the true cause of the trigger. When something happens to you or you have someone's words leave you feeling upset, hurt, angry, annoyed, enraged (or any other emotion), the fastest way to discover which deficiency story is driving this scenario, is to use the Boomerang technique. A boomerang is a traditional Aboriginal tool that is thrown and (with skill) it returns to you. It is similar to how your deficiency story casts a line into the world and reels back in a scenario that matches that story.

You might have heard people say that the external world reflects the internal world. Everything that is happening outside of you stems from your sense of self and your identity, which is that framework of beliefs, including your deficiency stories, and core deficiencies. When you don't feel good enough, you seem to attract situations that tell you you're not good enough. When you feel like a weirdo, like you don't belong, you tend to have experiences in your life where you seem to be rejected and unaccepted. The world outside of you responds to the world within you, and that world can be filled with deficiency stories.

We are meaning-making machines. We receive an overwhelming amount of sensory information and energy input and at best, we make sense of it through our brain. We label things, we create beliefs, and we use mental concepts and structures to feel safe in a largely chaotic and unpredictable world. When we are triggered, often without realising it, we have made the situation mean something about who we are. It has pushed the buttons of our deficiency stories. Or, the scenario has activated the deeply hurtful stories we unconsciously or subconsciously believe about ourselves.

Using the Boomerang invites you to ask one simple question to help find the root of your trigger or problem. It involves listening with tender care to the meaning you have placed on yourself about the problem. Take a current issue, worry, stressor or scenario you have in your life right now. When you look at that issue, ask yourself, if it was to mean something negative about you, what would that be? Trust me, go towards the negative. Your answer could be 'I'm failing', 'I'm broken', 'I'm weak' or the like. This is the deficiency story that is driving the issue in your life. If you learn best via video, you can watch me explaining the Boomerang using these two QR codes:

Part One:

Part Two:

When you ask this question, either mentally or in your journal, it is not an analytical process using the thinking mind. It's an intuitive process, noticing what is sitting quietly under the surface. If you don't get a clear answer to your question, that's okay. Sometimes a clear deficiency story doesn't surface immediately. Sometimes, it's helpful to reframe the question to 'if this issue was to mean something about *life*, what would that be?'. Perhaps it means life is unfair or life is unsafe. See what naturally arises when you ask what it means about you or about life. This is how we can identify the stories that shape how we view ourselves and the world.

If you're not sure what your answer is to the Boomerang question, that's okay too. It can take time to hear the deficiency stories under the noise of our everyday thoughts. And sometimes, no answer arrives. Yet the more we explore with this question, the more our deficiency stories begin to reveal themselves.

Be aware of self-beratement and blaming yourself for causing all of these bad situations and events in your life. You might think it's all your fault because everything stems from within you but the truth is, you are human. Being human includes creating a sense of deficiency, a sense of lack, whether it's regarding lack of safety, lack of receiving love or lacking being enough. Every single human being has felt negative about themselves or deficient in some way. Every human being is triggered and feels uncomfortable, whether they know it or not. Everyone has felt 'less than' in their lives.

None of this is your fault.

Both my internal and external worlds were a mess. I felt like one big black hole, and every time I tried to make life work for me, I got chewed up and spat out like a disgusting piece of nothing. And I *felt* like nothing. I felt stupid, a failure, loser. I wasn't good enough. Learning how to identify what was driving this endless cycle of horror for me was like being given a handrail to walk myself to freedom.

During the COVID pandemic, I was mortified to see on the news that a mother had been separated from her newborn baby for four days. She had given birth in New South Wales and her son had been transported by air to the emergency unit at a Queensland hospital. While she was told she would have the necessary paperwork to get through the border checkpoints to meet her son in hospital, this wasn't the case. As I was watching the news report, I was absolutely livid, like something inside of me was crawling beneath my skin. I couldn't sit still. I couldn't sleep. I was propelled to post my disgust of this news on Facebook.

After practising some natural rest, I asked the question: 'If this situation was to say something about me, what would it say?' Intuitively, I heard the words: 'I'm not heard', and I saw the picture of the mother in my mind. Then in an instant I had a rapid succession of flashbacks coming through my mind of the day my daughter Ivy May was born and then rushed by ambulance to Melbourne Hospital from Castlemaine without me. Without Leigh. Without anyone she knew. Ivy had been having trouble breathing, and a sea of a medical team had swamped what had been our safe, quiet, and sacred birthing suite to take Ivy. There was no space for any family member to travel with her. My most vital and primal needs as a mother to hold my freshly-birthed, warm and delightful newborn were cast aside and I was left alone in what then felt like a cold, big and empty hospital room. In those moments, my needs as a mother were not heard. My intense reaction to the woman on the news being separated from her newborn son was driven by my own separation from my newborn daughter.

Next time you're triggered, practise some natural rest and with the situation in your mind, ask yourself 'if this was to say something about me, what would it say?' or 'if this was to mean something about me, what would it be?' When waiting for your internal response, practise natural rest and wait for the answer to present itself naturally, in its own time. Don't try to force the answer. It will come. Let the words naturally rise to the surface. Be aware that the answers that do come might trigger you even more or make you cry. *Allow* yourself to cry, and then keep reading so you know what to do with the words that come. That's the next incredible step to dissolving depression.

Nervous System States

Understanding the basics of modern neuroscience can help us understand ourselves and our mental health. With the help of our nervous system, we engage in the world in a state of protection or connection, and we survive and thrive. While two of our nervous system states are well known – 'fight and flight' and 'rest and digest' – polyvagal theory shows there is a third nervous system state, which is referred to as the 'freeze and please' state. The fight and flight nervous system state is for mobilisation, the rest and digest nervous system state is for connection, and the freeze and please state can be described as disconnection.

Within the nervous system there are two branches: the parasympathetic nervous system and the sympathetic nervous system. Within the sympathetic nervous system, the fight or flight response is activated. It helps us move to defend or flee a situation that threatens our survival.[14] While modern-day living doesn't see us being chased by lions, we have more subtle threats like trying to meet a deadline, hurting someone else's feelings or making a mistake at work.

There are two branches within the parasympathetic nervous system: the ventral vagal branch which offers the rest and digest response, and the dorsal vagal branch which offers the freeze and please state. The rest and digest response helps us to feel calm and safe when there are no threats. In the rest and digest phase, our bodies can afford to expend their energy on normal bodily functions like digesting food and we feel safe to connect and engage socially. The freeze and please mode can activate when the body has used up all of its resources to fight or flight. If we experience stress, trauma and distress *regularly*, the body can move into a 'soft freeze', dulled or lethargic state which can then lead to depression.

At secondary school, after my parents had separated, my teachers noticed a change in my behaviour. My French teacher would say, "when Bronte doesn't understand something she shuts down. It's like she puts a wall up". It was because it hurt too much that I didn't understand. I thought it meant that I was dumb, not smart like the girls at the front of the class. I thought it meant there was something wrong with me. It was easier for me to muck around and blame the teachers for my disengagement.

Sometimes when we have a distressing experience, the dorsal vagal branch of the parasympathetic nervous system can naturally become dominant to find safety. This is the body's ancient way to 'play dead' as a way of survival. The body shuts down. When you move into the freeze response, not only can you become low in energy and motivation, you might also feel shame, want to be isolated, find it hard to express yourself, and withdraw.

During a distressing experience, you might feel helpless and freeze. This can lead to dissociation where you are disconnected from your body, your emotions and your life. You might have out-of-body experiences as a way of coping or feel like you're watching your life happen instead of being *in* it. Learning about how the nervous system works helped me regulate it and it made me realise I was dissociated for many years.

When I lived with a significant adult in my life, I felt trapped and helpless. I didn't feel like I could express myself without being put down. Whatever I did or said appeared to be wrong in this person's eyes. I felt like I was hounded at dinner time and treated like I was nothing.

Even when I tried to behave in a way that I thought would be acceptable for this person, that was wrong too. There would be a condescending smirk, a patronising remark, sometimes it was irrational outbursts of anger towards me and on the odd occasion, physical intimidation. It got to the point where I chose to keep quiet because anything I said was going to be wrong and I was going to cop it. I would think to myself, *What's the point in talking? I'm only going to get shut down.* I became silent in my own home, and dissociated from myself and my body.

Despite this turbulent relationship, fighting and fleeing the situation wasn't an option. If I fought, I got into trouble for being rude and disrespectful. If I fled, which I pondered from time to time, I would have been homeless. So, in order to survive, my body naturally relied on the 'freeze and please' response. I went quiet, said nothing, and told myself no one cares and I didn't matter anyway.

If we don't feel safe in a relationship with another, we can enable submissive behaviours. An experience as simple as crying as a child, and not being cradled or cuddled to help self-soothe can activate the freeze or please state. We can begin employing people-pleasing tendencies and put others' needs before our own in an attempt to receive more love, attention and care from others. Subconsciously, we can think as children, Mum and Dad don't want me crying, I must stop crying. This can be the start of emotional repression.

Science now shows that our nervous systems pick up on the nervous-system states of others around us. When young children experience a threat, their nervous systems become dysregulated and move out of the rest and digest state. Caregivers who are in a rest and digest state and physically hold, care for, nurture and love their children, helps their child's dysregulated nervous systems return to a rest and digest state. This is called co-regulation.[15] The children regulate their nervous systems with the adults' nervous systems.

Whether we are children or adults, we are biologically affected by each other. When we see a loved one is moody, we can feel it in the room. We might also start feeling moody – it rubs off on us.

For every waking minute of our lives, our bodies are moving in and out of nervous system states to help protect us or connect us. And our hearts are respectively closing and opening. This all boils down to how safe or unsafe we feel in the environment, situation, conversation or experience we are in.

Our nervous system states are not clear cut, they work together. You might feel a slightly activated fight and flight state with a tight chest if you think about your overloaded to-do list. And with clear planning, you might return to a state of calm and feel in control. Perhaps you're in conversation with a good friend and for the most part you feel safe in their company but as soon as they embark on talking about something you wish to avoid, you might feel a subtle shutdown, where you don't know what to say. These automatic states your body's nervous system moves in and out of, helps you be ready to protect yourself when you feel unsafe, and move into a deeply satisfying connection when you feel safe.

I always thought there was something wrong with me when I went blank if someone had a go at me. But all this time, this was my body's way of ensuring I was safe. I had moved into a subtle freeze state. All this time, I hated myself for always agreeing with other people and not daring to share my independent and differing opinion for fear they wouldn't like me. I told myself I was weak. But this was my body's intelligent way of making sure I was protected.

All that time, I had no control over my 'freeze' reactions. These nervous system responses are automatic. They happen before the mind engages. I realised it wasn't my fault, and it wasn't because I was stupid. In fact, all that time, it meant my body was working for me, protecting me, helping me to feel safe. What a relief.

Trauma

I always wondered why I had depression when 'nothing really happened to me'. Sometimes I look back at my life and think the things that happened weren't 'bad' enough and that I should have been able to get over things sooner. I would doubt myself and think surely I should have just gotten over it like everyone else. I certainly didn't put myself in the category of having trauma.

The Oxford dictionary defines trauma as: 'a deeply distressing or disturbing experience'. Yet trauma experts point to trauma being the *reaction or response* we have to the distressing or disturbing experience. A traumatic experience is personal. It's not an objective event but a *subjective* experience. It's what we make the situation, event or scenario mean about ourselves or life rather than a factual event. A traumatic experience happens within us; it's felt through our bodies and it's real in our minds.

Let's look at where trauma starts. In our everyday lives, our nervous system is constantly receiving information from our external environment. We're taking in smells, sounds, tastes, sensations and visual cues. Neuroception is the process of the nervous system picking up cues from the external environment before any thinking happens.[16] All of this information is sent to the brain so the mind can form meaning (or a story) about it. This becomes our subjective perception of reality. But when we experience something deeply distressing, the nervous system and brain become so overwhelmed with an overload of information and energy, the brain and body fail to make sense of it all.

Leading trauma specialist Dan Siegel explains trauma as an experience that overwhelms our capacity to cope.[17] During a traumatic experience, the threat is so big that we can't process the information. The rational brain is affected, and our executive functioning goes offline. This is when we can't think straight or make clear decisions. To help mobilise the body to either fight or flee from the situation, cortisol is released. This hormone impacts the function of the hippocampus, which is responsible for memory. Increased cortisol decreases the integration of memory, and particularly emotional memory.[18] This leaves us failing to remember what happened but more importantly, it leaves emotional memory unprocessed, or trauma stored in the body. Unprocessed emotional memory (or trauma stored in the body) is what you might call your baggage or pain. Trauma binds to the nervous system. This is what we carry around with us when we don't have the resources to process and integrate it.

After a traumatic event, when we haven't processed the experience, our nervous systems remain in what is called an incomplete trauma cycle.[19] This means the body remains in a hypervigilant or shutdown state, ready for more threat, thinking that the traumatic event is still happening. The body doesn't know the traumatic event is over. With any trigger, or small cue from the external environment, the nervous system might respond as if it is a major threat. We can see this in our everyday lives when we look at the numbers of people living with anxiety.

When we think of trauma, our minds often go to rape, domestic violence or war. These are horrific experiences and I want to acknowledge, not diminish them. At the same time, I want to acknowledge that *everyone* has been through a traumatic or distressing experience that has caused pain.

Experts in the field refer to Big T and Little T.[20] Big trauma. And little trauma. Big T is something as intense as rape, domestic violence and war, and there is Little T too.

Everyone has a story worth telling. Everyone has horrible memories they want to shut out. Everyone has past wounds. Everyone has experienced trauma. No one comes out of life unscathed.

Gabor Maté describes trauma as not what happened to us, but what happened inside of us as a result of what happened to us.[21] The moment a Grade 6 boy hissed "sufferrrrr" to me on the way into the classroom when I'd fallen up the steps as a little Preppie; this wasn't a meaningless event for me. My whole sense of safety cracked into a million pieces, and I felt small, scared, unsafe and vulnerable in a big, busy school. From an onlooker's perspective, it might not have looked traumatic or distressing but in that moment my whole world fell apart.

Whatever distress or trauma you have experienced, I am acknowledging your courage to live with each one of them. Your life has been hard. Painful things have happened. Maybe it feels like no one understands how hard it has been. I hear you. I welcome you in your struggle to make sense of what has happened. The tools I will soon show you can help make sense of and manage that trauma. You might be in tears. I feel your pain. But you're not broken. With tender care, your past experiences can be resolved.

This is where we misunderstand our children. We forget that our logical and rational perspective on our children's problems is vastly different to the raw, emotional experience our children are having when their whole world has just broken into pieces. I remember being consoled when a girl in my netball team was teasing me and intentionally excluding me. I was given advice on how to stand up for myself and make sure I was included in the half-time circles. Practical strategies had me physically a part of the team, but my real problem was the sheer pain I felt being excluded, like I didn't belong. I felt like an outcast. Tossed aside as if I wasn't part of the team. I felt like I didn't matter. I carried a lot of pain revolving around that exclusion, and until my KI sessions, I didn't know how to process that pain.

In our culture, we are quick to want to get over it and get on with things. But these 'small things' that happen in our lives build up and deep down, they can feel soul-destroying. When I was depressed, I felt I was expected to just pick up as if nothing happened and move on.

Our society thinks that we have to have been through Big T to warrant mental illness. But it can be subtle, ongoing little T's like degrading remarks from someone close that leaves us feeling unsafe and disconnected from ourselves, the people around us and the world around us.

It's not your fault that you haven't 'gotten over' your life experiences. Your brain and body have been doing their best to help you survive from the threatening situations you've experienced. Your entire system has been working hard to keep you safe ever since.

For too long, mental illness has been viewed as an issue from the neck-up. Treatments for mental illness have primarily focused upon mind-based therapies like changing your mindset. But we forgot about the whole of our being. New studies on trauma and the brain show body-based (or somatic-based) methods where we tend to the nervous system, best treat trauma.[22] If you're somebody with mental illness who hasn't been improving by talking through your problems, the latest science points to why.

Leading trauma expert and psychiatrist Bessel Van Der Kolk, who has dedicated his career to finding the best treatments for trauma wrote in his book, *The Body Keeps the Score*, 'Psychologists usually try to help people use insight and understanding to manage their behaviour. However, neuroscience research shows that very few psychological problems are the result of defects in understanding. Most originate in pressures from deeper regions in the brain that drive our perception and attention. When the alarm bell of the emotional brain keeps signalling that you are in danger, no amount of insight will silence it.'[23]

Back in 2009, a year after Mum had died, I confided in a colleague that I had depression. She responded by sharing that her sister had depression too. My colleague expressed her agitation with her sister for having depression because nothing bad had happened to her. She told me she could understand why I had depression because my mum recently died. She was frustrated that her sister just couldn't get on with things. At the time, I felt too much shame to tell her that I had been suffering depression long before Mum passed away. At the time, I thought I wasn't any better than her sister, having had nothing much happen to me other than my parents divorcing, being teased at netball, and having a difficult adult-child relationship.

Let me show you how you can end up with depression from a series of distressing or traumatic experiences. Mental health specialists explain there are a range of traumas including acute, developmental, preconscious, generational, complex and more.[24] Acute trauma is a single, threatening experience that activates our fight or flight sympathetic nervous system. From this experience, we more than likely create a deficiency story about ourselves in the moment such as, 'I'm not safe', 'I'm not good enough' or 'I don't belong'.

Developmental trauma is the result of ongoing distressing experiences that build up and place the nervous system into a state of stress over a prolonged period. When we don't process the words (thoughts and stories), memories, and emotional memory from these experiences we end up carrying a whole heap of baggage around, and we can't bear to look at it or feel it. These ongoing distressing experiences act as reminders, more confirmation and evidence to solidify our original deficiency stories. We find ourselves believing these stories to be true, believing them to be facts. We can feel the truth of these stories in our bones.

Ever since I formed the story that I am a 'bad girl', I had that story return again and again, and had it play over and over in my life. When someone didn't like what I said, I told myself I was bad or that I had said the wrong thing. If someone was upset with me, it was my fault for having done the wrong thing, that I was bad. And if I had made a mistake that had hurt, upset or agitated someone else, that meant I was bad too. This accumulation of multiple 'bad' experiences solidified the story and sense that I was a bad person. Learning KI started to resolve this trauma and had me stop feeling, behaving and believing that I was a bad person.

So how do we move out of a state of constant threat for survival and return to a place of calm, rest and homeostasis? How do we feel safe within ourselves and with others? How do we undo the damage? And how do we stop stacking up more pain in the body? The way to complete a trauma cycle, process our thoughts and emotions and return to safety is to use resources to *integrate* the experience. When we have someone to show us how to stop and safely turn towards the stories (words) of our painful memories (pictures) and learn how to connect and feel the associated emotions (sensations) that arise with those stories and memories, the trauma cycle completes. Our emotions process and we start to feel more connected, present, and embodied. We feel lighter, freer, clearer. We feel safe within ourselves and find a sense of home in our own bodies.

Co-founder of somatic-based approach to healing trauma, Embodied Processing at the Centre for Healing, Ryan Hassan helps us find acceptance in life's inevitable challenges. He says: "trauma is a part of the human experience. We're all on a spectrum. And part of the human experience is coming out of protection and into connection. The more we start to deal with this underlying survival drive the more we open up to connect with ourselves and our fellow human beings which then makes us feel safe."[25]

Just imagine if every human being on the planet knew the tools to manage their own trauma, come out of protection and into connection. If the simple act of feeling our feelings was celebrated in our culture, imagine what our world could look like.

CHAPTER FOUR
What We Resist Persists

The attempt to escape from pain, is what creates more pain.
- Gabor Maté

Months before my depression dissolved, I had a mental health nurse tell me bluntly (unknowing of my own battle with mental illness) that people who are depressed don't know how to feel their feelings. Ouch! After twelve years of personal development and two decades of meditation practice, I thought, *you're telling me I don't know how to do something so simple?* As much as it shook me, I absorbed her words.

I didn't know how to feel my feelings. Well sure, because if I felt my feelings I would die. Many people had told me over the years to feel my feelings but the sheer thought of feeling my feelings had me rooted in terror. When you're in the grips of depression and you're spiralling at a rapid rate in what feels like a big black hole, the most debilitating fear is that you won't ever get yourself out.

In 2008, I had my psychologist suggest my fear of feeling my feelings was worse than the actual feelings. For a few moments in a session with her, she tried to help me feel my pain. But I couldn't. It would hurt too much. I feared I would get swallowed up by it. That door was shut, and I wasn't opening it. Ever.

It took me another thirteen years before I was shown how to safely feel my feelings. Hopefully, since you're reading my book, you don't have to wait the thirteen years I did. What I found in my discovery was that rejecting my feelings created my biggest struggle. If this is too much to comprehend right now, and if you have resistance to this concept, I hear you. The thought of our feelings are horrible, hard, and can be horrific. For now, I ask you to trust me and to consider that there might be a possibility to feel safe as you feel your feelings.

You might be freaking out right now even contemplating feeling your feelings. Undertaking what feels like a monumental task, feeling your feelings can require explicit teaching, guidance, and one-on-one support so you feel safe at any given moment. So you experience your feelings slowly, gradually, and you get to choose how far you go.

It's not your fault if you're frightened of your feelings. You are a product of your environment. When you're five and another child has ripped your artwork, your well-meaning teachers and educational support workers are rallying around you telling you not to worry, and that you can create another piece of artwork. When you start school and you're terrified about going in on your first day, your parents are telling you that you're okay, you're brave and that you can do this. When you're dumped by your first boyfriend, your friends are telling you it's okay and you're beautiful and they didn't deserve you anyway. The way we are supported is to be whisked away from the pain of feeling how bad we feel, and making things better with taking positive action for the future. No dwelling on emotions allowed.

The problem with this is that we are always running from our feelings and not developing skills to be comfortable with the full experience of being ourselves.

Everyone is saving us from feeling pain by finding solutions and answers to fix our problems.

When you're depressed, do you feel like everyone is trying to fix you and make you feel better? And does that make you feel worse? Have you ever wished that everyone stopped giving you advice and actually just *heard* you, *listened* to you and allowed you to be sad? When I was depressed and given advice I felt even more like a hopeless case who couldn't get their shit together.

In a world of phone addictions, an ever-increasingly fast-paced lifestyle and productivity-hungry society, slowing down to feel your feelings is radical. Many would argue, why would we want to feel bad when we can feel good? Well, perhaps the suicide and mental illness rates are a strong indicator that pushing forward to feel good all the time is not the answer.

The last time I checked, human beings experience a broad spectrum of emotions from ecstasy, bliss and passion, to rage, grief and sadness. No one is immune from emotions. As a society, we have completely dismissed an inherent part of our experience.

While we find emotions elusive and something we can't grapple with, simply put, emotions are sensations with a label attached to it. You might feel a sensation through the body that you would label 'happy'. You might have a different feeling in your body that you could label 'sadness'. Perhaps you experience the body feeling 'frustrated'. Emotions are experienced in the body through sensations.

You will find that I refer to feelings and emotions as body sensations. There is too much of a negative connotation with feelings and emotions, and they feel too complex for our minds to understand. But I'll say it again, feelings and emotions are simply sensations that have a label attached to them. See how noticing and feeling sensations is much less scary than feeling feelings and emotions? So I will continue to refer to feelings and emotions as sensations, because that's all that they are.

This is what was missing for me all along. This is the step I wasn't shown at school. We have been taught to be proactive and do something about our problems without ever feeling the sensations. We've been taught how to run from the bad feelings and run to the good. We've lost our ability to live within the full spectrum of what it is to be human.

The general concern is that if we stop and feel our feelings, we might not ever get ourselves out of there again. We might stay stuck in the mud, be in a rut forever and never get going again. So we plough through life, exhausting ourselves until we are so burnt out we can't muster anything else. We work ourselves to exhaustion until we have no choice but to collapse. We are so terrified of feeling, that we've formed generations of communities who believe that it's weird or wrong to be emotional and don't know how to allow ourselves the simple act of feeling.

One profound moment proved to me that our answer is to simply turn inward. After a long and tiring day on my own with the kids, one evening as they played in the bath, I felt explosive rage. After asking them many times to use quieter voices in the echoey bathroom, my eldest – Jackson – yelled out in playful delight one time too many. I felt a red, ferocious surge rise through my body and I was on the verge of yelling and screaming at him.

Instead, I caught my voice just in time, and turned the direction of my propelling rage away from him. I didn't suppress it but put my full attention on the intense hot and rising sensations in my body. In a miraculous moment, this red and unpredictable rage morphed into overwhelming beauty. In one full second, accompanied by only gentle awareness and delicate precision, I sat staring in awe with love for my child. My body's intelligence naturally settled the intensity, and the rage was gone.

This moment showed me that the answer to all our problems is to stay with ourselves. Rather than trying to work through our problems, we are to find out what's driving the problem. Rather than keeping our emotions hidden and staying positive, we are to feel them so they process and clear. Rather than spilling our mess onto everyone else around us, we are to take full responsibility and hold our mess with love.

When people would tell me to feel my feelings, I thought I would die but when I was shown how to practise KI everything changed. My KI Facilitator took me by the hand and showed me how to feel safe with my emotions. If you're nervous about going to this next step with me, I welcome you as you are. Know you can just watch from the sidelines as I show you how to feel your feelings without dying in the process.

The worst part about life is that often it shows up in a way we don't want it to. And often, we feel a certain way that we don't want to feel. Maybe you're feeling crap, out of sorts, or not yourself. Maybe you said something you didn't really mean or acted in a way that you didn't really want. Maybe you wished you hadn't said something to someone. Maybe you wish you didn't have depression. All of these are every-day examples of how we resist life as it is.

The thing that really makes us struggle is that we are not allowing what is already here, to *be* here. Life is showing up in ways we have no control over, and we refuse it. We are fighting something that is inherently *here*. We can't change the colour of the sky, we can't change what people think of us, and we can't change that we look a certain way. Resisting life as it is, creates the real struggle.

But I get it. You don't want to accept life as it is because you want it to be better. You don't want to accept a mediocre life when you can have a magnificent one! If we accept life as it is, there is a concern we might miss our full potential and not achieve the most amazing things in our lives that we know, deep down, we are capable of. The problem with never accepting life as it is right now, is that you miss the most inherent peace and freedom that comes with surrendering to *right now*.

You're really not alone resisting your own feelings. There are only eight billion other people on the planet resisting them too. We humans try to escape our emotions every day. In fact, we are obsessed with staying positive and doing anything to avoid what we perceive to be negative feelings. Our boys think it's weak to cry, our teenage girls get picked on for having 'PMT', our men keep their feelings bottled up and only let it out with alcohol, and our women learn that in order to be taken seriously, their emotions are to be left at the doorway of the board room.

No one wants to feel crap. Sometimes, we wake up feeling off, dragging our feet to make a coffee to get going. Kids might be in our face when all we want is some peace and quiet. We might feel hopeless compared to the picture-perfect posts on our feeds. And other times we're faced with a day of exhaustion meeting everyone else's needs when we're running on empty.

When we're not feeling bright and like ourselves, we wonder what's wrong. We think, *what did I do to get here? Or what didn't I do?* Enter self-beratement: I can't even look after myself, let alone after everyone else. I should have gone to bed earlier; I should have done that job already; I should have gone to yoga; I should have gotten off my phone sooner. When we feel out of sorts, we don't accept ourselves for all that we are, including our thoughts (words and pictures) and feelings (body sensations).

There are so many painful memories in our lives that we don't want to think about. It hurts. Deep down, these memories tell us we're weak, horrible, bad, ugly, wrong, not good enough, dumb, an idiot, not smart enough. And sometimes there are no words for it. We just know we don't want to go there. It's too painful.

When feeling low, I would see the girl in my netball team who bullied me flash in my mind and my mind's eyes would try to put the light out on her. I'd cringe at the sight of her. She was tall and lanky, fair skin, blonde hair and often ignored me. She tried to exclude me from half-time huddles or avoided partnering with me for practice drills.

One Monday night training session, she scoffed at me and turned to our team mate laughing as she said, "all she needs is glasses". She meant I was the epitome of a 'loser'. While the rest of the girls confirmed this with laughter, and the coach made a terrible attempt to hide her own smile, my world crumbled inside. Every time I saw that girl in my mind and that scene at netball training, I was reminded I was a loser.

When we have bad memories enter our minds, we quickly block them out. We don't want to revisit them. It's too risky, too painful. It's better if we wipe our minds and redirect our focus onto something good, something positive, something uplifting. The only problem is that the dark memories continue to stack up, bubbling over the edges until we can no longer escape them. They come billowing up and out until they are screaming at us for attention. They haunt us when we are alone. And when we feel bad all the time, constantly chasing the good is exhausting.

But what if we could just stop running? What if we safely sat with the memories that were here and found a way to feel our feelings without being terrorised and retraumatised? I'm so pleased to tell you there is a way to do exactly this. Just imagine what your life would be like if you could stop running from that looming, deep, dark depression. What would life be like for you if you didn't need to block out any painful memories or hurtful words? Imagine if you didn't have to escape your own emotions and felt safe to feel them instead? All of this happened for me when I learnt to use the Kiloby Inquiries.

When we are escaping our emotions, we are really escaping ourselves. It doesn't matter where we are, our emotions come with us. If you stop to think about it, the idea of us trying to escape our emotions is so absurd! What are we thinking?!

As a wider society, we don't celebrate the full expression of being human. If we cry in public, often we will be apologetic about it, we will wear sunglasses to cover our tears, or only cry in the shower or behind closed doors or say something like "I don't know why I'm crying!" Even though crying is a natural biological process that offers deep healing, a cleanse and release, it's deemed as a shameful process and not accepted as a part of our everyday life.

When I was depressed and cried, I often thought I was 'falling apart'. This story made me cry more. Crying, for me, meant that I was not coping and that there was something wrong with me. That I wasn't keeping up with everyone else around me and was being left behind. Those three words 'I'm falling apart' were on autoplay whenever I cried or whenever I was sad. This story kept me in a looping cycle of self-pity and self-loathing… which made me cry even more.

When we see other people crying, it's uncomfortable for us. We don't want to see them in pain. We want to prop them up, make them feel better and fix them so they feel good again. As a society, we have lost the ability to be present within the full spectrum of emotions from ourselves and from others.

Perhaps it's the pace of today's world, the instant gratifications, external solutions and quick-fix consumerism that has left us impatient, unprepared and unwilling to have anything that's uncomfortable stay its course. Staying with our feelings – whether our own or someone else's – takes time, patience and slowing down.

When someone comes to us with a problem, we jump to wanting to solve things for them. We're not interested in *hearing* them. We feel a sense of responsibility, that it's our job to help them feel better. We don't want to see them suffering, whether it's because we are sensitive to others and we don't want to get dragged into their negativity or just don't like them being so sad or feeling so awful. Maybe we can see how truly amazing this person is when they themselves can't, and we want them to see what we do.

Either way, we are not accepting them as they *are* in the moment. In this very moment, they are flat, negative, drained, and in pain. For us to fully accept them as they are, would be to accept them in their flatness, negativity and drained pain; to allow them to be as flat, negative, drained and in as much pain as they are. *This* is unconditional love. Giving this person full permission to be just as they are without the need to change. The more important question is, can we sit with the discomfort that we feel in our own bodies as we watch them in pain? If they feel better, we feel better. So when we are trying to fix them, we are really trying to escape our own selves. Our own discomfort.

The message I received from the world was that it was 'bad' to cry. My teachers 'there-there-ed' me until I wasn't crying and others gave me action steps to take to make things better. But all I wanted was someone by my side who let me *be* just as I was. I wanted someone to accept me for who I was without the need to be something different, without the need to be 'fixed'. The more people tried to fix me, the more broken I felt. And the more broken I felt, the more I retreated into my deep, dark world of thoughts.

Mum was the only one who, on occasion, let me cry. I remember crying for hours in her company because I was filled with self-loathing, believing I was ugly due to the acne on my face. I felt detestable and tried to hide myself. I didn't want people to look at me and be disgusted by my presence. While I felt relieved Mum just let me cry, it was a welcomed relief to learn how to feel *pleasure* through crying via the Kiloby Inquiries.

It's not only when we are in pain that we escape our own feelings. We escape our feelings every day, and most of the time we're unconscious to it. We'll make ourselves busy so we don't have to feel how it feels to wait at the lights or for the kettle to boil. We'll fill our schedules so we don't feel lonely or bored. We'll use spirituality, overachieving, food, drugs, alcohol and our phones to keep ourselves from just *feeling*. Have a try. See how long you can sit on the couch without anything to distract you so you can just feel how it feels to be in your body. Something this simple can feel so painstakingly boring, threatening to our minds, and impossible.

The problem with escaping ourselves day-in and day-out is that we never fully experience the freedom, beauty and pleasure of living with ourselves. When we are trying to escape ourselves and our feelings through addictive habits and tendencies, we spend our entire lives fearing ourselves. We run from ourselves and miss the gift of simply *being* ourselves. Imagine what life would be like if you felt comfortable in yourself, by yourself, in your body, in your skin, in relationships, in social situations, and in your current and future phases of life.

If you're on a spiritual path, you might have used positive affirmations or intentions to raise your vibration, uplift your spirits and feel better. Yes, our thoughts create our reality yet at the same time, we can't deny our body's feelings. When you have depression, it doesn't matter how many times you affirm that you are 'abundant', stating affirmations won't take your painful un-abundant feelings away from your body. Speaking positive affirmations when you're feeling horrible is like putting a sparkly unicorn band aid over the top of a pile of shit that is oozing from underneath your skin. Feeling your feelings brings a sense of peace beyond what any positive affirmation will ever offer.

In 2007, when I studied Reiki and learnt about energy work, I tried releasing rituals to let go of what no longer served me. I would plead with the full moon, traditionally a powerful time to let those parts of us go that we are ready to be rid of, and it never worked. I would get so angry with the universe for not taking away the horrible feelings within me. Now that I feel safe to feel my feelings, the power of the moon gracefully sweeps up the debris that's left, rather than taking away my pain. Later you'll see why the moon not ridding me of my pain was a gift.

I grew just as frustrated with grounding techniques. I'd have my bare feet on the grass, wishing for the crap to leave my body so I could have some kind of relief from the pain inside me. I was resisting the parts that were mine. I didn't want to feel them. I just wanted them to go away, and I was irritated, grounding my energy wasn't helping. Once I got comfortable feeling my feelings, I understood what grounding was on a deeper level, which I will share with you in Chapter Eight.

In 2015, one psychologist introduced me to cognitive behaviour therapy (CBT). It involved me recording my behaviours, actions and thoughts for the challenging situations and scenarios I had experienced the previous fortnight. I had to record the thoughts I had at the time of the incident, the actions I took, and the thoughts that might have been better to have about the event rather than the original thoughts I had at the time of the event. This process was essentially trying to flip my statements from negative to positive.

On good days, I felt inspired, empowered and invigorated to write new potential thoughts if that situation happened again. On harder days, though, I felt like a failure that I couldn't think so positively all the time. What was wrong with me? Having to rewrite my automatic thoughts about a difficult situation to more positive thoughts left me feeling like I couldn't even get thinking right! Never have I heard of someone automatically thinking positive thoughts when something goes wrong. We are human and we naturally hear stories in our minds that are full of self-doubt about ourselves or the situation we're in. Rewriting statements never got to the bottom of my depression.

Attempting to change our thinking is like trying to rewrite our mental programming without going to the control panel. Trying to swap our thoughts for other thoughts keeps our mind busy and keeps us away from the real issue. The root of the issue is how the deficiency story feels in the body. That's what makes it an experience we would label challenging, uncomfortable, and negative. But when we feel so safe with our stories and feelings, then there's nothing we need to run from.

When we are trying to change our habits and behaviours through our mindset only, we are not even scratching the surface. Our deficiency stories are what drives the same problems in our lives. No amount of flipping beliefs is going to make a difference until you clear the body of its emotional memory. If you have a belief or deficiency about yourself that is stored in the body, you will remain in a looping pattern of the same issues, in a different scenario perhaps and with different people, but the same issue.

In my life I noticed that I never really felt like I belonged. I didn't feel like I belonged at school, at netball, at Uni, at work, and the backpackers when I was travelling, nor at home for family Christmases. Anywhere and everywhere I went, I felt like I didn't belong. This was my core deficiency story – 'I don't belong' – running the show. This was driving and creating scenarios in my life that matched that story. Dropping into my body and surrendering to the physical *feeling* of not belonging was my answer.

We can fall into escaping ourselves through overachieving too. In the first two years of running my business, I ran myself into the ground trying to be the next Gabby Bernstein. I'd built the Soul Worker Academy, a premium online school for women to feel clear, confident and courageous pursuing their path of sacred service. I'd started writing a book and had my eyes set on a Hay House publishing contract, I'd spent a healthy portion of my business income on video marketing to make me a star, and my social media following was growing rapidly.

The only problem was that while my business looked amazing, my personal life was completely out of balance; my house was a mess, I never saw my husband, I wasn't present with my kids, I was on Facebook all day and I wasn't living in line with my environmental values. I was so driven to become a star that I couldn't stop.

If I stopped, I feared I would be a no one, a nobody, I'd be alone, I'd be missed like I often felt as the third child. Most of all, I feared I wasn't enough. I was escaping myself and my core 'I'm not enough' deficiency story. All of that overcompensating, all of those achievements I was making, was never enough. It never felt like enough because deep down I never felt like enough.

Even meditation and mindfulness can be an avenue to escape ourselves. A drug of choice. Something that will numb the pain. For many years I used meditation to escape my difficult world. I would go on guided, intuitive or meditative journeys and experience a shift in consciousness that had me feel bliss, euphoria and an overwhelming sense of oneness. Until I left my meditation pillow and got smacked in the face by life the next time I was triggered. It was an endless cycle of what felt like falling apart to chasing some kind of feel-good feeling before falling apart again. And so the cycle continued. It was exhausting.

Both meditation and mindfulness helped calm my nervous system, but it never addressed the root of my pain – the deficiency stories formed during those significantly distressing events in my life. Basic mindfulness and meditation simply wasn't enough to dissolve my depression.

At the time, I didn't expect meditation to be my cure. But now as I reflect, there was something missing for me. I wasn't truly receiving the support I needed to resolve my mental illness. The Kiloby Inquiries is more than basic mindfulness. They are advanced mindfulness techniques, or applied mindfulness, which I will explain in Chapter Seven.

Now that I no longer need antidepressants, I can see that I used medication to escape myself. The pain I felt was too much. It was too scary, and I didn't know how to stop it. Antidepressants saved me when I was at my lowest. They stopped me feeling an overwhelming sense of dread inside. At the time, I didn't have the somatic awareness, nor words to articulate my depression. But this pain that felt like too much, was essentially dread. Intense dread of being me. Self-loathing. Not wanting to be myself. Wanting to be someone else or somewhere else. Escaping my intense sense of dread was my answer until I found the tools to stop resisting and start allowing.

Surrendering and allowing were concepts I was used to on a spiritual path. The Kiloby Inquiries gave me a practical framework to apply it in a practical sense to my depression.

We can continue to escape ourselves in a myriad of ways, whether it's through spirituality, overachieving or addictions, whether we are escaping our memories, emotions or depression itself. Perhaps we find temporary relief through resisting our full spectrum of human expression. We can try basic mindfulness, meditation, mindset work, CBT or something else to support us through depression but for me, none of these got to the bottom of my depression.

Depression, or feeling depressed, is being weighed down by a build-up of deficiency stories attached to emotional memory or physical sensations in the body. The only way out of depression is through the body. After all those years talking about my problems to my counsellors and psychologists, going around in circles and getting nowhere, all I needed was for someone to take my hand and show me how to feel safe with my feelings.

In order to feel safe to feel our feelings, befriending the mind must take place first, which is what I will show you how to do in the next chapter.

CHAPTER FIVE
Befriending The Mind

*"When we believe what we think,
when we take our thinking to be reality, we will suffer."*
- Adyashanti

Knowing my core beliefs was helpful because it gave me an understanding of my makeup. But by the fiftieth time having another mental health professional tell me I had a core belief that I wasn't good enough, my silent yet exasperated response was *'Well now what? What do we do now that we know that?'* My psychologist or counsellor would continue on as if we were making progress, but I felt like a broken mess and that there was something wrong with me because I couldn't shake the core belief. I was stuck with it forever. Knowing my core belief didn't make it go away.

Enter Simple Inquiry. Simple Inquiry is the foundational practice in the Kiloby Inquiries and the practical step you take to unhook yourself, layer by layer, and disidentify from your core beliefs or deficiency stories. I will be referring to this practice throughout each chapter. When I say, 'take it to Simple Inquiry' I mean to process your thoughts and emotions using this practice.

Many meditation teachers, Buddhist or spiritual teachers often guide you to 'look at the thoughts', 'welcome the thoughts', 'let the thoughts come in and go out'. It poses many questions:

- how do we do that when the thought, belief or core deficiency story is so painful that we want to block it out?
- how do we look at thoughts when there are so many spewing from deep within us and it feels like there is no end?
- how do we look at thoughts that keep looping and looping over and again?
- how do we actually look at our thoughts?!
- how do we stop ourselves from ruminating in our heads, and spiral into our own mess when we look at the negative thoughts in our minds?

The next two chapters answer all those questions. And it opens the door for you to feel the freedom that comes from facing the pain, fear and dark from which you've been running. There are two parts to Simple Inquiry: the mind and the body. This chapter will show you Part One of Simple Inquiry. You will find instructions and details on how to unhook from the thoughts in your mind using Simple Inquiry and additional techniques you can weave into your Inquiry practise including Focus Shifting, Pendulation, Tapping and Tracking.

The next chapter will give you Part Two of Simple Inquiry. It will show you how to process the emotions in the body that have been attached to your thoughts.

Simple Inquiry shows you how to look at, welcome and feel safe to be with all of the parts that make up your negative story. One section at a time. Think bite-sized chunks. Remember, your negative story is made of three things only: words, pictures and body sensations. When you practise Simple Inquiry, you use different techniques to feel safe looking at the words, the pictures and the body sensations.

This simple technique is a process of looking from a place of compassionate awareness and acceptance, watching or witnessing from a distance all of the parts that make up the deficiency story. We start by looking at the words and pictures or the top layer of Velcro. And once they have dissolved, we feel the sensations in the body, which is the bottom layer of Velcro. When we can be with all parts of the story – one part at a time – the story dissolves, the emotional memory or feeling attached to it clears, and we don't identify with the story as much. It's like the story becomes water off a duck's back.

This technique is a game-changer. I have given you four introductory paths: detailed explanations through Chapters Five and Six, along with how I benefited from the techniques; a training video; a video demonstration; and guided audio. If you can practise Simple Inquiry, you will know how to free yourself of all of those stories you are sick of hearing on loop in your head.

Simple Inquiry video training

If you learn best through video, use this QR code to access training on Simple Inquiry from my online course, Beyond Belief. It's comprehensive. You'll need an hour. You might like to take notes.

Simple Inquiry video demonstration

Use this QR code to watch a video demonstrating how to practice Simple Inquiry with a Kiloby Inquiries Facilitator:

Simple Inquiry audio guide

Click on this QR code for an audio that will guide you through some basic mindfulness or natural rest and then show you how to practise Simple Inquiry to manage your thoughts and process your emotions:

If you've watched the video and want to skip the written section on Simple Inquiry, skip the instructional sections in Chapters Five and Six.

The first place to begin practising Simple Inquiry is from a place of natural rest. Remember, this is when you feel calm and relaxed. It is when your mind is open, aware and curious. If we practise Simple Inquiry when we're stressed about a problem, such as being useless, we can get stuck in the stream of thoughts and exacerbate the story, experience it as real and be in a worse position than when we started! Using natural rest, simple mindfulness or nervous system regulation techniques, help to return your body and mind to rest. Once you are resting you can begin Simple Inquiry.

Simple Inquiry – Part One

Let's take the deficiency story 'I am useless' as I guide you through the process of practising Simple Inquiry. Imagine you think you are useless. When you take this story as truth, you are stuck in your mess, or stuck in Velcro. This means the words 'I am useless', the pictures that go with this story, and the corresponding body sensations are so stuck together the story feels true and you see yourself as useless. You *become* the story and experience life as its truth. If you can't relate with this story, then choose another deficiency story you identify with.

Remember, there are three parts to this story. The words are 'I'm useless'. There might be memories of you feeling useless or memories of people telling you that you are useless, either verbally or nonverbally. Memories are mental pictures; these are the pictures that go with the words 'I'm useless'. And finally there will be body sensations that go with these words and pictures. You might feel heat rising through your shoulders, neck and face or feel prickles on your arms. When the words, pictures and body sensations associated with 'I'm useless' are stuck together, this story feels true for you.

See the words and the pictures

To help you absorb this information easily, we'll focus on the words first. The words are one of two parts to the top layer of Velcro.

Start Simple Inquiry with your eyes closed. Imagine you have a movie screen before you. Put the words 'I'm useless' (or your chosen story) on the screen. Shoot the words up there and plaster them on the screen. Start to see how the words look. Are they written in capital letters, lower case, or both? Are the words big or small? Are the words written in a particular colour? Are the words displayed on the same line or is it one line of words above the other? Where are the words positioned? Are they in the centre of the screen, to the left or to the right? Are the words close or far away? Are the words parallel from you or angling away? Are the words in 2D or 3D? Really see the words.

If the words 'I'm useless' are too painful to look at, choose a deficiency story that doesn't have as much of a charge. Remember, you are learning a new skill here. Go easy on yourself. But choose a story that you want to disidentify from.

Notice the space

The words on the screen are surrounded by space. Follow these steps:

- with your eyes closed, draw a rectangular frame around the words with your finger in the air so you can see that the words are inside the frame
- put your attention above the framed words and you'll see empty space, where there are no words
- then bring your attention back to the words to see how they look
- shift your attention to the space below the words
- then look back at the words to see how they look
- put your eyes on the space to the left of the words
- then look at the words to see how they look now
- now put your eyes on the space to the right of the words
- then look back at the words

You can even put your eyes on the space between you and the words. When you look behind the words there is space. There is even space between each letter. Noticing the space around the words and letters can help you feel safe having the words there, especially if they have a strong meaning for you.

You might notice that when you shift your attention between the words and the space, the words might have shifted, changed, morphed, faded, dissolved, moved further away, gotten smaller or bigger or stayed the same. All are welcome.

Next, take the time to notice the intricate detail of the words

Start to watch each letter of each word with interest and curiosity, like you've never seen these letters strung together before. Imagine these words are like a glorious piece of artwork on a wall in a gallery and notice the intricate detail of each letter. Look at the corners, the edges and the curves that make up each letter. As you look, these letters might shift, change or stay the same. Again, either or all of these are welcome.

Watch the words dissolve

Finally, as you rest with the intricate detail of these words and allow yourself to be with the words in a gentle, loving space, these words will fade, dissolve, and clear in their own natural way. Once you can no longer see the words, it's time to bring your attention to the bottom layer of the Velcro. These are the sensations in the body.

Come to the body

As soon as the words are no longer visible, take a deep breath in and as you breathe out, envision a mini-you sliding down from your head, through your throat and into your body. Start to find a safe place in the body where you can imagine yourself sitting. This safe place is where you can begin to explore, feel, and connect with the sensations in the body. With your attention and skilful Inquiry, these sensations and the bottom layer of Velcro of the story – 'I'm useless' – will clear. We will go into working with the sensations in depth in the next chapter.

Before we go there, let's investigate Focus Shifting, processing pictures and troubleshooting when the words look stuck.

Use Focus Shifting to help you feel safe and stay focused

You may feel apprehensive looking at these words or get lost in the myriad of thoughts coming and going. Focus Shifting is a great technique to apply to help you feel more comfortable and safer when looking at these words, and help you stay on track. Focus Shifting is when you shift your attention between the words and the space around the words.

- start by holding both hands in the air on either side of the words
- as you breathe in, look at the letters of the words
- as you breathe out, look at the space to the left of your left hand
- as you breathe in, look at the letters of the words
- as you breathe out, look at the space to the right of your right hand

Repeat that process and notice what happens to the words. Every time you put your attention on the space, look at the space as if that's the only thing that exists. And every time you return your attention to the words, notice with curiosity how the words look and see if they have shifted or stayed the same. Either way is perfect. To watch me explain Focus Shifting via video, please use this QR code:

If the words are starting to shift, fade, reduce in size or morph into something different, sit back, relax, grab your popcorn and watch the show before your eyes. Use gratitude to have the words feel loved and received. Verbally say "thank you" to the words for being here. Tell the words they can stay for as long as they'd like. Tell them that you love them. (Yes, I am asking you to speak aloud to words in your head.) Trust me. Do it and notice how the words respond to your care and generosity.

Practise surrender. What you resist persists. Lose any agenda of trying to get rid of these words. When you find yourself wanting these words to go away, they are likely to stick harder or stay longer. The acceptance of what's here, and allowing the words to be here will help them soften. As you relax with the words, they will relax too.

Hold compassion for the words

Treat them as if they are the greatest gift you've received today. Because they are! Witnessing these words is like waking up from the dream-state and realising you are not the words.

See these words as a newborn baby. Hold your hands on either side of these words and imagine gentle and warm love emanating out of your hands for the words to absorb. Notice how the words are responding to the love from your hands. These words are an aspect of you that have merely wanted to be loved, heard, witnessed and held. Let them receive all your love.

In allowing the words to be here, they tend to lose their charge. If the words started as angry or frightening, your sense of love and acceptance naturally diminishes ferocity, harsh meaning and the spewing power these words can hold, until they begin to fade.

By creating a gentle loving space for yourself and the words, the words can become jumbled, or it might look like the letters start dancing playfully or they might morph into a picture. When we take the time to look at the words, they have their own way of creatively expressing and transmuting themselves on their own. Without any effort required. The key is in simply allowing them to be there.

If you practise these techniques and think they are crazy and a potential waste of time, you're not alone. I doubted it myself. I thought the techniques were weird and wondered if it was really going to fix my depression. But I trusted the process. I was committed to following the steps. And it worked. The first time I practised Focus Shifting, the letters started to fold up, get blurry, get smaller, roll into a ball, dissolve and fade into nothing.

Before practising Simple Inquiry, I had words that I feared would kill me if I looked at them. But my KI Facilitator showed me how to look at them in a safe way. I started to see these words that had held so much debilitating meaning for me, for what they really were. Words like 'you're a hopeless case that no one can fix' became merely letters strung together. These words that had held me captive for so long were merely sounds put together to make words.

In a strange way, looking at the words I had feared for decades was like a non-event, an anti-climax. Here I had been terrified, trying to escape the stories: 'you're falling apart' or 'you're a loser'. But the moment I stopped and looked them in the eye, all I found were lines and curves and edges and corners that made letters. I almost felt robbed! Surely my pain was more than this! But when I looked, that's all I could see.

Surely these horrible words that had me constrained in the most horrific pain were more than a series of letters. But all I could find was interesting symbols that we call letters. I was looking at letters and words with fresh eyes, with a beginner's mind. In this space of allowing and being curious and inviting myself to rest with both the space and the letters and words, the charge and horror fell away, the words didn't mean so much to me and they certainly weren't painful like I always thought they were.

Now let's focus on processing the pictures

When you think about being useless, maybe there are particular people, bad memories or potential future projections that pop into your mind. These are mental pictures. Maybe the people in your life keep popping up when you wish they would go away. Perhaps you try to block the memories so you don't have to feel the pain that comes with it. Maybe the worst-case scenarios haunt you from the background, hiding in the shadows of your mind as a lurking energy, leaving you feeling exhausted from fear and anxiety.

But what makes a picture? When you look at a picture, it's made of colours and formations, curves and lines. Sometimes there are objects in the foreground and things in the background. There might be faces of people, silhouettes or whole bodies in the picture. Without the body sensations that go with your memories, they are simply mental pictures. It's the coupling of the sensations with the pictures and the words (or story) that make it real, meaningful and painful.

Return to imagining you have a movie screen in front of your eyes. Think of the idea of being useless and see what pictures present in your mind. It might be a picture of a person, a memory or something else. Shoot that picture or pictures on the screen in front of you. Start to see the picture there. Notice the different parts of the picture. Be curious and look for which colours are in the picture. Look at the different shapes and formations that make up this picture.

Notice the space around the picture

See where the picture ends. See where there is 'picture' and no picture. Draw or put an imaginary frame around the picture so you can see that you are decidedly looking at a picture that is outside of you. You are not 'in' the picture. This helps you avoid reliving a memory.

Notice the space on the outside of the frame. Shift your attention between the picture and the space. See that there is space above, below, to the left and to the right of the picture – just as you did with the words. Notice there is space between you and the picture. See that there is even space behind the picture. You might see the space behind the picture start to seep through the picture.

Use Focus Shifting

Look at the corners of the picture, the edges, and the parts you haven't fully looked at. Then start using Focus Shifting.

- raise your hands to hold the picture between them
- breathe in as you look at a new part of the picture
- breathe out as you put your full attention on the space to the left of your left hand
- breathe in as you look at another new part of the picture
- breathe out as you put your attention on the space to the right of your right hand
- repeat this process

Every time you breathe in, look back at the picture with interest to see how it looks now. Notice if the picture looks the same or if it's changing. Lose any agenda of trying to get rid of the picture, and just rest with the picture as if it's the greatest gift you've been given today.

They are your greatest gift! These pictures are those that have been stuck to the sensations we call trauma and pain in the body. The pictures have been stuck in the body and holding the sensation there. When the pictures and words arise, celebrate!

You can't know what's there until you see it. Being consciously aware is the first step to healing. When you see the words and pictures come, it's a gift because they are on their way to being cleared and released. It's a joyous celebration! They are coming to the surface to have light shine on them. Once the pictures are dissolved you are one step closer to healing the trauma in the body. Then you feel lighter, clearer, like you're no longer carrying around a heavy weight everywhere you go.

Use Gratitude Statements

Just like the words, the more you want a picture to leave, the more it will stay. Memories hold all the power when you are terrified of looking at them. Using gratitude, such as saying to the picture "Thank you for arising. You're welcome to stay for as long as you like. I love you", helps your nervous system know you are safe, and the picture begins to lose its power.

Give a heartfelt "thank you for arising" to the words and pictures. Give them full permission to be there, and say "you're welcome to stay as long as you like" and "I love you". Say it aloud to these words and pictures. Allow them to be in the space in front of your eyes on a screen or in a picture frame. Notice how those words and pictures shift, change, fall away, fade, dissolve, collapse or fold up in some creative way! Use this QR code to watch my explanation on using gratitude statements:

If the words look stuck and they're not changing, this is when Tapping and Tracking come in handy, which I will show you soon.

Keep your eyes open to help you stay focused

Maybe you're someone who doesn't like to have their eyes closed or perhaps you find it difficult to stay focused looking at words in space! I think for anyone starting out, these techniques are so foreign it doesn't necessarily feel easy. What you can do to help you stay focused (or feel safe) is look at the words and pictures on a blank wall. Instead of closing your eyes and putting the words and pictures on the imaginary screen in front of you, shoot the words onto a blank part of the wall in the room you are in. Check the usual detail of the words: if they are written in capitals or lower cases, big or small, 2D or 3D, on one line or multiple lines. And notice the shapes, colours and formations of the pictures. Putting the words and pictures on the wall as you keep your eyes open is helpful when you're tired, and keeps you on track.

If you can't see the words, listen to them instead

Some people can't 'see' words when they put them up on an imaginary screen. If this is you and you're feeling like a complete failure because you can't do it, you haven't failed. Don't give up. The first questions to ask are: 'Do you have a sense of the words? If you had a sense of the words, what would they look like?'

If you don't have a sense of what the words would look like you'll be able to hear the words in your mind. You might even hear them in someone else's voice, which is worth exploring too. When you can only hear the words, use this audible version of Focus Shifting.

- At your own pace, mentally repeat the words you can hear in your mind. Eg. 'I. Am. Useless'

- As you breathe in, listen to the sound of the words as if you have never heard them before
- As you breathe out, listen to the sound of silence as if it's the most interesting and fascinating sound you've ever heard. Put your full attention on the sound of silence
- As you breathe in, bring a bucket of curiosity and notice how those sounds (or words) sound now
- As you breathe out, listen to the sound of silence
- Repeat this process, with interest, as if those sounds are the greatest gift you've been given today
- Once those words no longer sound like words, like you can't really make sense of the sounds, your next step will be to take a deep breath and come to the body

If the words sound stuck, use clicking, which I explain a little further on.

Sometimes I can see words clearly and other times I can't. When I can't, I use this technique to listen to the words. Interchanging techniques of looking at words and listening to words can help you stay focused without getting lost in mental distractions like what you're going to cook for dinner!

Use an open focus

When we are dead focused on a picture of a memory that has caused so much pain and don't apply techniques to help us feel safe, we can accidentally begin to relive this painful experience as if it's happening again right now. Looking at pictures and words with an open, relaxed focus, rather than a closed, tunnel-vision focus is one of these techniques that feels safe as it softens the rigidity and intensity.

When we welcome the pictures and words as well as the space around them, we are resting our awareness on all parts of this experience. The pictures and words don't feel so intimidating or threatening. We see there are pictures and words, which might feel threatening, but there is space too, which is typically non-threatening. Our attention on the space helps to soften and then dissolve the pictures and words. Sometimes it looks like the space moves into the picture and words and then you are left with nothing.

As you look at the picture, check in with your body to see if it is at rest and relaxed. If it's relaxed, great! If it's tense, that is okay too. This is your body's natural way of ensuring you are safe. You haven't failed if your body is full of tension as you look at words or pictures. Rather than berating yourself for having tension in your body, see if you can let that part of your body be tense. Give it full permission to be tense. Hold loving space around the tension and when you're ready return your attention to the picture, do so slowly, with love, patience and a gentleness. Your nervous system starts to unravel and the body begins to realise your distressing experiences are over and it doesn't need to be stuck in a survival response. It can relax.

Practise Pendulation when you feel unsafe

When you feel unsafe looking at words or pictures, space can be your refuge. And space is ever-present. When the words or pictures look threatening, start to see the edges or boundary where the pictures or words end, and you will find space. The space is a gentle, restful place you can come to if the words and pictures are too much.

You can spend *more* time looking at the space than the words and pictures if you like. This is your practise, and you get to decide what works for you. Play by looking out of the corner of your eye to the words and pictures for a split second before coming back to resting your attention fully on the space for an extended period until you are ready to look at the words and pictures again. Or if it's too much to look at the picture or words itself, you can sense that those words and pictures are there as you keep your eyes on the space. This gives you time to feel more comfortable with the words and pictures without needing to look at them directly.

If a child can't swim, do we throw them in the deep end? No. That would be traumatising for them and completely unsafe. We would invite them to sit on the edge and get comfortable with the water, ask them if they want to dip their toes in and playfully splash the water. Once they're comfortable in their environment they feel safer, more prepared and ready to be fully immersed in the water with some floatation aids or adult support.

The same thing goes for being with words that feel painful, pictures that are traumatic, and body sensations that are terrifying. Being asked to talk about our problems and past is similar to being thrown in the deep end when we can't swim. First, we need direction to identify all of the parts of our problems and triggers – the words, pictures and body sensations. Next, in order to feel safe to be with all those parts, we need supportive guidance and clear, practical instructions to feel safe with them when they arise.

Use Tapping or Tracking for words and pictures that look stuck

While some words fade before your eyes with love, attention, breath and space, others don't! Some words have been buried deep in our subconscious or have been ignored and blocked from our mind for so long that by the time they arrive centre stage on our imaginary screen, they don't want to go anywhere! They want all the love. All the limelight. They want to be seen. Heard. Witnessed. And loved. Some words we put up on the screen look stuck, as if they are going to stay forever. This is when we can use Tapping and Tracking.

Tracking is the process of moving your attention between the words and pictures and the tip of your moving pointer-finger. This helps soften and dissolve the words and pictures that look stuck. If the words or pictures look stuck:

- open your eyes
- move your pointer finger in a random pattern in front of your face, similar to how you would if you were drawing something in the air
- watch the tip of your finger as if it's the most interesting thing you've ever seen (as if nothing else in the world exists)
- keep looking at your moving finger for about five seconds
- look back at the words and pictures to see how they look
- repeat this process and notice how the words and pictures respond

Typically, Tracking reduces the intensity of the words and pictures and they become easier to look at. Eventually, the words and pictures start to soften and dissolve, fade or leave in their own unique way. For me, Tracking works every time, very quickly. If you'd like to watch my explanation on Tracking via video, please use this QR code:

Tapping is another great tool to have up your sleeve when the words and pictures look stuck and refuse to budge. Here's how to do it:

- look at the words and pictures on the screen
- start tapping on your forehead just above the bridge of your nose
- as you tap, imagine that you are tapping on every single part of the picture or words
- when you tap, verbally repeat "thank you" to the words and pictures
- once you have tapped on every single detail of the words and pictures, keep tapping
- put your full attention on the sound and feeling of your finger tapping on your forehead
- once your full attention is on the sound and feeling of the tapping, stop tapping

Every time you tap on every single part of the words and pictures it's like you are blessing each part. If you don't enjoy the feeling of tapping on your forehead you can tap in the air as if you are tapping directly onto the words and pictures that are on the screen. If you missed my explanation on tapping via video, please use this QR code:

When you say "thank you" to a picture of a person who has hurt you, remember you are saying thank you to the *picture* for being here, *not* the person.

When pictures of people who have hurt you arise, it is the greatest gift! When they rise to the surface to be looked at and tapped on, these techniques will help you feel free of being triggered when you think of or see that person. Practising these techniques will help you feel relaxed when you're in that person's company. Just imagine being in the same room as the people who normally trigger you and you feel safe to be yourself. Without your guard up. Without your protective masks on. Just being you. This is what the Kiloby Inquiries bring. This is freedom.

Use an audible version of Tapping

If you are someone who can't see words on the screen but can hear the words, you can replace tapping with clicking. Here's how you do it:

- start by listening to the words as you repeat them in your mind
- breathe in as you listen to the words
- breathe out as you listen to the silence after the words
- repeat this practice

- start clicking your fingers with each word or syllable as you continue mentally repeating the words on your in-breath
- listen to the sound of no-clicking, or silence, as you breathe out with no words
- every time you breathe in and click, notice how the words might sound different or the same
- repeat this practice at least three times

After a few rounds, you'll likely hear the sound of the words start to shift and lose their charge and eventually the words will become inaudible. Once the words are inaudible, you can stop clicking, take a breath, and then come into the body to feel.

So far, I have shown you how to befriend your mind and unhook from your deficiency stories, beliefs and thoughts using Simple Inquiry and other techniques. The next chapter will guide you through the second part of Simple Inquiry – how to process emotions in the body that have been attached to your deficiency stories. I trust the combination of written instructions and explanations, audio and video guides has helped you digest the techniques. If you don't completely understand or know how to practise these techniques, I was in the same position as you. To be honest with you, I didn't completely understand nor see the value in these techniques until I experienced a one-one-one session with a KI Facilitator so they could show me how to practise KI. Until then, follow me into the second and most juicy part to Simple Inquiry.

CHAPTER SIX
Body Intelligence

Trauma is hell on earth. Trauma resolved is a gift from the Gods.
- Peter Levine

While the last chapter was all about processing the mind's thoughts through befriending its words and pictures, this chapter is about integrating and processing the body's emotions. In this context, integration is when the body and mind become connected, trauma is completed, and the emotions are processed. Integration is the opposite of dissociation, or a disconnection with the body. Not only will I introduce you to more of the techniques that dissolved my own depression, I will also reveal a hidden treasure inside of you that you may not have known existed. It's profound.

Simple Inquiry – Part Two

After the words and pictures have dissolved, begin by taking a deep breath. You have taken the top layer of Velcro away, which leaves you with the bottom layer of Velcro. Taking a deep breath between working with the top layer (words and pictures) and the bottom layer (sensations) helps the mind stay focused on the practice. It signals to your brain that the first step to Simple Inquiry is finished and it's now time for it to direct its focus on the body.

Take a deep breath and find a safe place in your body

When you take a deep breath, use your out-breath as a way to slide down into the body. Imagine you have just shrunk into a mini-you, your throat has turned into a big slide and your mini-you jumps from the top of the slide and glides down into a safe place in your body. Where you have the whole place to yourself. No one is around. Notice where your safe place is. It may change, but for now, this is a place you can return to at any time.

Feel the sensations in your body

From a place of rest, say hello to your body. Start to feel into the sensations in the body. Start to notice which parts of your body are calling for your attention. Notice what body parts want to speak to you. Maybe you notice your right shoulder is tight or there is a feeling in your legs that you can't really put into words or it feels like there's a ring around your hips. Sensations come in all shapes and sizes all throughout the body. Start feeling.

At first, your patience might feel limited to sit and feel. With practise, your ability to feel more will grow.

Develop a connection with the body through curiosity

Here, in this safe place, you can imagine your mini-you looking at and investigating your body. Welcome a sense of playfulness and cheeky curiosity and see your body like the best playground your inner child has ever found. Explore the different parts of your body with your 'feeling-eyes' from different angles.

Locate a sensation that is calling your attention

Once you've located a sensation in the body, rest your quiet attention on it. Start to notice it and feel into what it's doing and how it wants to express itself. Inspect to see whether it is still or moving, pulsing or constant, gentle or intense pressure, pulling or swaying, or something else entirely. Check into the sensation to see if it's stabbing or aching, tingling or buzzing, burning or heavy, hard or soft, or something else. Verbally describe how it feels to help your mind stay focused and attentive. Feeling our feelings is not something we have typically learnt from our parents or teachers so be gentle on yourself to develop this skill. It takes some time and practise and, with my help, I know you can do it.

Find the space around the sensation

Then notice that this sensation, however it is expressing itself, is surrounded by space. First, locate the boundary of the sensation. For example, if the sensation is in your chest, how high does it reach? Does it go right up to your throat? Or is it only in the middle of the chest? Where is it positioned exactly? Welcome it as it is. Find the perimeter where the sensation ends and put your attention outside of the sensation to find the space. Put your 'feeling-eyes' on the space above the sensation, below the sensation, to the left of the sensation and to the right of the sensation. See if you can open your awareness and notice both the sensation and the space in your body at the same time.

Play with these techniques as you read this. Check into your body now and start to notice what sensations you have. If you can't feel anything, here's a gentle reminder that joining a yoga or basic mindfulness class can build your mind-body connection and increase your interoceptive awareness.

Accept the body as it is

Most of the time if we feel pain, tension or aches, we immediately want these sensations fixed and gone. But this 'need to fix' all the time exacerbates our suffering. Often, we see these sensations as a threat. But I am here to tell you that the stories you might have about these sensations are more of a threat than the actual sensations. Your thoughts could be making mountains out of molehills! *Rather than trying to release tension, see if you can let them be as tense as they need to be.* Your acceptance of these parts of you will give them freedom to move, express themselves and process in the way they need to before leaving the body. Our instant reaction is to want perceived 'bad' feelings to leave but learning how to accept yourself, including the body's sensations, clears mental stress and repressed emotional baggage.

Try going *with* the sensations as they are rather than trying to make them change. Some sensations can be tight and knotted, tense and contracted. See if you can make those tighter. Some sensations will feel really heavy. Make them heavier just by looking at them. Some sensations might feel like they are burning. See if you can make them burn more. Some sensations will feel big. See if you can make them bigger. Play with giving these sensations full permission to be just as they are.

Sensations can feel really scary. If you don't feel safe practising these techniques on your own, this is normal. It can take some gentle guidance from a KI Facilitator to create a space to feel safe with big, heavy, burning, painful and tight sensations before you can be with them on your own.

During the twenty years of having depression, I had a lurky-like feeling come through my body that would haunt me. It made itself known and threatened to take me under. I didn't have the emotional literacy for this feeling, but I called it 'my depression'. As I mentioned earlier, now I can identify it as dread.

When it would creep in, its subtle presence would rise from the pit of my stomach and reach over my shoulders to sit in my arms and neck. I didn't like it. Coupled with the sensations were the words 'there's something wrong'. I was stuck in Velcro. I constantly searched for ways to escape 'my depression'. But the moment I let that wave of dread come over my body, my depression collapsed.

In 2019, during the weeks leading up to when my depression dissolved, I received my first one-on-one KI sessions. In those sessions with my KI Facilitator, I had been practising welcoming my sensations rather than pushing away from them. Even though I still had the instant reactions of wanting to run from my pain in the fear that I would die, I was gradually building a capacity to remain open, call on the techniques when I needed them, and trust that I was safe.

In May of 2019, the moment my depression collapsed, I was in the middle of my kitchen. In the previous days, 'my depression' had been lurking and threatening to overwhelm me. I had kept it at bay by staying busy. The kids were bouncing around me as I was preparing lunches. The 'depression' was getting louder and closer. It really wanted to rise and take up my whole body. I remember feeling like I was standing at a crossroads in a timeless space. I had a choice to try and keep this intensity behind the wall of the dam or let go, face it and feel it.

I knew what I had to do. It was time to let the sensations come. I pep talked myself with 'you know what to do. Just use the techniques.' I deliberately put my hands on the kitchen bench to help me feel stable in what felt like a frightening few moments. With a deep breath, I opened my body up and watched this familiar yet immense wave of dread sweep through me like a tsunami. It rose from the pit of my stomach, filled my chest and throat. I let it come. And it kept coming. There were flashes of thoughts like 'you're going to die'. My body was full of intensity.

Then a moment later, something miraculous happened. The sensation of dread, the feeling I had labelled 'my depression' for so long, began to dissipate, settle, and then leave my body. It came and then it went. I couldn't believe it. After fighting this feeling for so many years. All I needed to do was to let it come and then it would go. I didn't drown. I didn't get swallowed into a spiralling black hole. I didn't die. That moment collapsed my depression. From then on, I could see that every sensation I would have labelled 'my depression' was simply a sensation. Since then, I have actively practised welcoming, loving, embracing, accepting and staying with the sensations in my body. And it has felt comforting, beautiful, and like coming home.

I never had depression after that. Don't get me wrong, I had sensations. I have had intense days with very strong sensations in my body, but the label 'depression' became irrelevant. I could now see myself as a human being who experiences sensations. Sensations are feelings. And feelings are for feeling. This moment of true liberation changed my life.

Use Focus Shifting

Just as we use the breath to dissolve the words and pictures, we can use the breath to process and clear sensations in the body. If you have a sensation that feels tight, stuck or dense, try breathing in the sensation and breathing out as you put your attention on the space around it. Stay with this process for a few breaths and notice how the sensation might be responding.

I am always amazed at how this simple technique softens, relaxes and reduces the sensation.

Work with multiple sensations

You might have more than one sensation in the body at one time. Perhaps there's a pain behind your eyes and a shooting sensation up a leg. See if you can hold your attention on both sensations at the same time. Hold space for both. Check in to see which sensation is calling your attention more. Which one feels stronger or has a greater pull? Which sensation feels predominant? Take your attention to that sensation. If there isn't one sensation that is calling for your attention more, then simply rest with both sensations. Sit back, relax and watch with your 'feeling-eyes' the ever-unfolding show of these sensations moving, morphing and expressing themselves in their own unique way.

Pull words and pictures out of the sensations

At first, there might be a lot of resistance that arises when you try feeling the sensations in your body. Maybe you have thoughts like 'I'm going to die', or 'I can't do this' or 'I don't want to have to feel this' or 'If I start feeling this black hole I might never be able to get myself out again'. This is what stopped me from feeling my pain for so long and it kept me trapped in mental illness for over twenty years.

If those stories are stopping you from looking at the sensations and feeling them, then put those words onto the screen to look at using Simple Inquiry. Work with the resistance first. Once the resistance has lifted, you will feel safe and ready to dip your toes into feeling the sensations.

When you notice a sensation that feels big, overwhelming or scary to feel, ask yourself if it feels safe to have this sensation here. If it feels safe then go with it, stay with it, feel it with interest and curiosity while noticing the space. If it doesn't feel safe, don't stay with the sensation. This can feel painful and scary. Instead, notice the words that come with that sensation. Are you hearing words like 'No, this is not safe' or 'make this go away' or 'I don't want to have to feel this'.

These are all words to shoot up onto the screen in front of your eyes. Use the same techniques as before: welcoming the words, looking at them surrounded in space, breathing in as you look with interest at the words and breathing out as you look at the space outside of the words. Once they've shifted, take a deep breath and return to the sensation in the body. As you check back into that sensation, notice how it feels now. Maybe it's changed or perhaps it's the same.

Generally, as we unhook the words and pictures from the sensation, the sensation's intensity starts to soften and relax and eventually the sensation dissolves.

Investigate further if the words and pictures feel irrelevant

If the words and pictures that come out of the sensation feel irrelevant, investigate further. Ask the word or picture if it represents something about you or life. What do they symbolise? Does it relate to you or your life in one way or another? Notice what answers come and add those words and pictures to the screen as well. Welcome everything, even if it feels irrelevant.

Use journaling to build mental awareness

Sometimes we have stories about our stories too. You might think 'There are so many stories' or 'I have too many stories' or 'When will the stories stop?' but these are stories too! When we start to raise our awareness of the stories in our heads, a running commentary starts!

If you've got too many stories, write them all down and then highlight the one that hurts the most. The one that hits you the hardest or has the most charge. Then take those words to the screen in front of your eyes.

Welcome gratitude practices

When a sensation stays, your most important role is to stay with it. It can feel very difficult to stay with a sensation you don't want to feel, that you're losing patience for and want to distract yourself from. The problem with this is that when we take our attention away from the unprocessed emotion it stays as baggage in the body. We keep carrying it around with us wherever we go! And it surfaces when we are triggered again.

Similar to acknowledging words and pictures with a sense of gratitude, try verbally saying to the sensation "Thank you for arising, I love you, I'm so glad you're here! You can stay here as long as you like."

These phrases help you turn towards the sensations. Then it softens and relaxes the resistance so it doesn't feel so frightening to have the sensation in your body. When you are using these techniques, remember you are doing BIG work! You are unravelling the nervous system out of a trauma-bound protection and into safety and compassionate connection. You are completing trauma cycles and finally learning how to feel safe feeling your feelings.

When I say these statements verbally rather than mentally, the sensation softens and dissolves quicker.

Treat your emotions as visitors

See your body as your home and see the sensation as a beautiful friend who has come to visit and stay. Play host and give this sensation everything it needs. Imagine sitting down with it and giving it a cup of tea. Give them the master bedroom and fresh towels. Have them know they are most welcome to take up all the room they want in your home.

This approach changes your relationship with the sensation. Rather than seeing it as something to get rid of, you feel safe to have it in your 'home'.

Were you ever taught at school that your body has its own intelligence to process its emotions? I certainly wasn't. It wasn't until I was shown how to be fully present and be in that watchful space and in an intimate relationship with the emotions in my body to realise that the more I got out of the way and the more I let my emotions guide me, the quicker the emotion processed and the lighter and clearer I felt.

I call this innate ability of the body to naturally process its own emotions independently and without the mind, Body Intelligence.

You can watch me explain Body Intelligence via video using this QR code:

When I had a strong emotion rise through the body, I watched it rapidly transform from something so intense and painful to immense beauty, peace and freedom. Once I felt a burning heat in my chest. My mind resisted with thoughts of it not being safe to go with this sensation, but I trusted the process and made the sensation hotter with my 'feeling-eyes'. In just a second, this burning heat in my chest transformed into utter beauty and had me in awe of the deep oneness I felt with being myself.

Another time, tears and emotions arose with memories of Mum. She passed away 11 years before I came off antidepressants. This was a long time to have been numbed from my grief for her. When I felt my heartache and that deep wrenching in my gut when I thought of her, I didn't want to go there. But when I relaxed and allowed the sensations to rise so they could be felt, I felt a deep sense of pleasure.

The Kiloby Inquiries showed me how to watch my body processing its own emotions independently. It didn't need me to do anything to help. It didn't need me to step in. It just needed the mind out of the way. I began to trust my body, and started to feel safer when my emotions rose through it.

I realised my emotions weren't a problem. They certainly weren't something I had to get rid of. I lost my need to raise my vibration or change my mindset to feel better about myself. I learnt to become present and felt content, happy and free to simply watch the ever-changing sensations, words and pictures that came and went.

Perhaps the collective story that we need someone outside of ourselves to fix us so we feel better, keeps our economy going. But does it help us thrive? My answer to this question is no. When we can accept, embrace and love the sensations in our bodies, we learn to feel safe. We don't need to run from ourselves. We learn to trust ourselves, our bodies, our emotions, our responses and our instincts. It builds a sense of self-sufficiency and empowerment where we don't need much outside of us. If we all did this, our natural world would look very different.

Be generous and open

Imagine your whole body is like a big body of water so the sensation has as much room as it wants to move and express itself. Give it centre stage! Watch the show and let this sensation fill your entire body with its presence. Love it. Tell it "encore!" See if it wants to stay where it is, dance, or move through your body. Hand over your whole body to this sensation so it has the reins and it can decide what it wants to do. You might see it moving from the heart area up to the throat and spread across your cheeks to your ears. Great! Let it do that! Then ask what it wants to do next. Maybe it wants to keep moving or maybe it wants to stay exactly where it is. Let it do what it needs to do.

If this doesn't feel safe, or if you have thoughts that say this isn't safe, pull those thoughts or words out and shoot them onto the screen in front of you to look at using Simple Inquiry.

When I hand my whole body over to the sensation, I tend to find the sensation wants to move. I get behind the feeling and celebrate it for expressing itself, deciding what it needs and moving in the way it wants. These are sensations that have likely felt stuck, hidden, constricted, bound and caged for years. Giving this sensation permission to move wherever it wants is giving that part of me that has felt caged, freedom. Every moment I am allowing my feelings to express themselves in the way they want, I am giving myself full permission to express myself in the way I want. I am healing myself in every single moment I am with my feelings.

When I say healing, I don't mean I'm broken or something to be fixed. Healing for me is a reconnection with and a reclamation with my true self. It's a realisation that I am complete, enough, and perfect as I am – nothing needs changing. I don't need to get rid of any perceived negative emotion in order to feel complete, good enough or okay. Healing is remembering that I am at one with all creation and the part of me that can see all parts of myself – words, pictures, body sensations, sound, breath, body, clothing, all of it – is my true nature. That part that is aware of all parts of life is my true nature. And I am not separate from those parts. I am that.

Let your feelings lead you

When a feeling is on the move in your body, let it move. See it as your teacher and your guide. Perhaps it wants to show you something. Maybe it wants to exit the body through your fingertips, your feet or out of your armpits. Or it might need to show you something. See where it wants to lead you.

Perhaps it will lead to something like a room in your abdomen or a door at the back of your heart. If something like this shows up for you, it's okay to feel nervous. You could ask "what's the worst that could happen if I entered that room?" and answers might intuitively rise to the surface like 'I'll die', 'I won't ever be able to get back out again' or 'I'll see the worst in me'. All of those words are words you can look at before you go into the room.

Once it feels safe, entering that room can be invaluable. You might be able to see what's inside the room. Or maybe there is some significance to the room. Maybe the room symbolises something for you. If it does, that will come in words and pictures. See how all of your answers will come in words and pictures? Simply look at all the words and pictures then feel the sensations. Always feel the body sensations.

One day, in a KI session, I was drawn to a tunnel-like cave in my body and I was petrified of what I would find in there if I looked. I had a sense that this cave was filled with all the bad things about me. They felt buried away in that cave so no one could find them. My KI Facilitator simply asked, "why don't you go and see what's in there?" After processing my fears by looking at the words and pictures, I entered the cave. I found nothing. Nothing was in there.

All that time. All those years I had been worried about people seeing all the bad things about me that were buried deep within. For so long I had had a sense that deep down there was something wrong with me and that I had to hide that. I was given the image of the cave and shown there was nothing in there! It was extremely liberating. I walked away from that session laughing at how I spent so much of my life worrying about people finding something bad but when I looked, there was nothing there!

This sense or feeling that we have about ourselves that we can't put our finger on can all be narrowed down to words, pictures and body sensations. It's the thought, and the sensation that goes with the thought, that makes things feel and seem really bad. But when we turn towards each part of the problem, one at a time – words, pictures, body sensations – they are all manageable. None of them are a real threat. They present and express themselves and then they leave. Nothing stays forever.

This was mind blowing for me. I had been so stuck in the mess of my head for so long, felt trapped going around and around in circles with my thoughts, but using these techniques showed me that every thought was a story. Like a picture story. An illusion. A perceived reality. Not the truth. A story. Made of nothing but words, pictures and body sensations. A *story* that had felt so real, palpable and inescapable. But with these techniques the stories collapsed, dissolved and dismantled in a matter of seconds or minutes.

Treat stuck sensations as gifts

Some sensations don't go away when you put your attention on them, love them and breathe with them. Sometimes they feel stuck and lodged, like they will never leave. There are two reasons why a sensation will stay stuck in the body: the sensation either has a purpose for being in your body, or it has a message to give you.

If it has a purpose or reason for being in your body, it will not leave until it has fulfilled its job. To find out what its purpose is you can ask it:

- why are you here?
- what is the reason that you are here?
- what is your purpose?
- how are you helping me?
- are you protecting something?

Have your journal handy as you ask these questions and write down the answers that come from the feeling. Whatever the answers are, they will be in words. The sensation won't go away until you have looked at the words attached to the sensation with love, compassion and acceptance. So put these words on the screen, watch them dissolve as you use the techniques, then return to the body. When you return, you'll likely find the sensation is less stuck, it's softer, lighter or less intense. Ask the questions that feel relevant and right for you again so you pull more words and pictures out of this sensation so it can keep processing and leave the body.

If a sensation has a message for you, it won't leave until you have received the message. The body is working for you, guiding you. We must know how to listen to it.

To find out what message a stuck sensation might have for you, ask:

- do you have a message for me?
- if you had a word for me, what would that word be?
- what do you want me to know?

Feelings are not a threat and not your enemy. They are your greatest gift. Imagine if we shifted our relationships with our emotions from 'I want this feeling to go away' to:

- thank you for helping me
- thank you for protecting me
- thank you for delivering my message
- this is perfect that this sensation is here

This attitude of gratitude shifts the stuck-ness of the sensation in the body and often it starts to dance and play with the energy you are bringing to it. It might frolic and dance frivolously in the space or may dart and shift between the throat and the heart.

Sometimes I can feel sensations that start as feeling so stuck and heavy and then spiral and move like a delicate ballet dancer that beams off the ground like the bubbles in a lava lamp. It's fun, light, effortless and free. Then the resistance to having this sensation leaves my mind and I feel complete and satisfied with this sensation here. There is no problem that this feeling is here. And just like a visitor leaves my home, so does the sensation.

Lose any agenda of trying to get rid of a sensation

Be wary of any need for this sensation to leave! The more you want it to leave, the more it will stay. It's like a defiant child who is not taking no for an answer. It will keep showing up until you love it, welcome it and say, "thank you so much for being here". In this surrender comes the peace and the freedom, where it doesn't really matter to you that the sensation is there. And that's when it leaves.

Use a child-like curiosity and playfulness

Welcoming a child-like curiosity to a sensation helps shift impatience and wanting to have a sensation go away.

See your inner child with big binoculars, peering through at the sensation from all angles and lifting parts of the sensation up so they can check to see what lies underneath the sensation. Picture your inner child dancing through and playing on the sensation and in the space around the sensation. Most importantly, check to see how the sensation is responding to this curious, child-like wonder and play.

While our minds can be impatient and just want the sensation to go away so we can get on with 'bigger and better' things to do, the body wants to be felt, loved, received and accepted as it is. These sensations are the parts of us we have abandoned, not had time for and not loved. These sensations are the emotions and feelings we didn't feel when they originally arose when we experienced trauma and distress.

These are the parts of ourselves we have tossed aside and rejected. When we take a radical step to turn towards those feelings we rejected, we are reclaiming the parts of ourselves that left us feeling broken. The more we meet all the parts of ourselves, including those sensations, the more whole we feel, the safer we feel, the more connected and more comfortable we feel in our own skin.

The more we stay with the full experience of being human, including the words, pictures and body sensations, the less lost, alone and disconnected we feel. There is no shame to be ourselves because we know all that is arising is body sensations, words and pictures. All of those can be looked at one at a time. We detach from the idea that we must have it altogether and realise the beauty, freedom and peace that comes with the ever-changing flow of the human experience.

Build your patience through basic mindfulness

It takes time for emotions to process. Emotions need time to express themselves and offer their gifts before they leave the body. Patience is required to be able to watch an emotion process naturally through Body Intelligence.

If you are having trouble staying present with an emotion that just won't go away quick enough, try returning to a basic mindfulness or meditation practice and build your capacity to remain in that practice for a longer duration. This will improve your ability to be patient, open and loving with a sensation that is taking longer to process and clear from the body.

When I stopped my medication and started to experience the fullness of being with myself, being human with all of the words, pictures and body sensations, I had some extremely intense days. When I was in the thick of life's pain, I couldn't feel the rising sensations in my body because the stories in my head took over my experience. The never-ending flood of voices rolled in as deficiency stories, grief and sadness, anger and hate, confusion and overwhelm. It felt like my head bounced between memories that linked the exacerbating stories.

On those days I couldn't work out what was right, what was wrong, whether I was a hopeless case, weird or different (in a bad way), and I started to doubt myself again, thinking there was something wrong with me. One story would be overtaken by the next and it felt like I was drowning in a sea of words about how bad I was as a person. A bad sister, bad friend, bad mother, bad person. Annoying. A burden. In the way of everyone. Horrible and selfish.

In those moments, I felt different. I felt like *I* was different and that the average person didn't have these crucifying thoughts about themselves. I looked at other people around me and they didn't seem to be welling up with tears at the drop of a hat like me. And I would 'argue' that maybe I did have depression and maybe I should be on antidepressants. Using a label like depression or mental illness made the intensity of emotions and screaming thoughts in my head make sense of this inner chaos. But at the same time, that label never took my depression away.

On those intense days, the screaming sensations and thoughts in my head felt like too much. Too much. Too hard. These were the words that kept me stuck in depression before I took antidepressants. During the twelve years of taking medication, I didn't experience these intense days because the antidepressants numbed me.

Sometimes I thought, *I don't want to be here.* The intensity was too extreme. On those days, I had full empathy for people who commit suicide. I thought, *hats off to those people who have lived with the megaphone of horrific stories about themselves being hammered at them from all angles of their mind for so long before taking their own lives.*

When I would struggle in my mess and turn to someone for help, their well-intentioned counsel often left me feeling like there was something wrong with me. I wanted to yell and scream at them for not understanding what it's really like. But I didn't. Instead, I mentally surmised that they would never understand how bad this was, which left me feeling alone.

Being depressed is awkward. It's surreal and strange when your whole body wants to explode with tears and life on the outside of you is all systems go, just as normal as it is every other day. Everyone around you is talking about the weather and other surface chit-chat while you are doing anything and everything possible to contain the dam of tears that are flooding your body. This immense jumble of body turmoil and spiralling negativity had me not knowing where to turn because no one had the right thing to say to me, no one could take my pain away and I was left wondering how to fix myself. Medication was my answer for many years.

But then I started to see that the emotional turmoil and negative thoughts were surfacing – to be looked at, felt and released. I realised that this blanket experience of intense emotions that I termed 'my depression', was a gift. Whatever the situation

I was in and however I was being triggered, it was the deficiency stories and accompanying sensations that were rising to the surface to be seen, welcomed and loved. When my body and mind screamed at me for attention, all they needed *was* my attention. My depression was a result of me ignoring the parts of myself that I had abandoned.

These moments with undying tears, a massive lump in my throat, my yearning to scream for help and my whole body wanting to explode, were the moments to turn toward myself rather than turn away and escape. Wanting all of what was in my mind and body to leave was what made it excruciating. Turning towards and loving every piece, one at a time, is what softened, relaxed and dissolved it all. I realised my depression – made up of words, pictures and sensations – was my medicine. The parts within me I had rejected were all I ever needed, all I was ever looking for.

When I practised and practised and practised, looking at each set of words, pictures and body sensations became easier and easier and my life became a devotion to staying with myself, being with myself and allowing myself to accept, love and embrace all parts of myself, including the body sensations, words and pictures.

I don't say I overcame depression because it wasn't something I got over. I wasn't so strong that I conquered it. It's more true to say that I let go enough that it dissolved. I didn't jump over my depression to get to where I am now. I never left myself or escaped my depression. The depression collapsed, dissolved and folded up neatly around me. All that time, it was nothing more than words, pictures and body sensations stuck together. And with time, looking at each word, each picture and each sensation in the body, the intensity of each became less and less. Until I didn't need something like antidepressants to take the intensity away.

The all-encompassing umbrella experience of depression started to unravel very quickly, and I started to see that what I was really experiencing was emotions, or sensations coupled with words and pictures. And when I could be with all those at once, independent of each other, I felt safe, and my depression dissolved.

During COVID lockdown I had a list of friends whom I felt abandoned by for various reasons. Within a short space of time, two people never got back to me to organise our next catch ups, one didn't respond to a business-related request, and one defriended me on Facebook. I felt very lonely and unlovable. I had the stories 'no one wants me' repeat in my mind and I felt like I had no friends. I was in a dark place. I was very sad and in the midst of drowning in daily motherhood of three young children.

I felt alone.

I finally sat myself down to practise some KI with my feelings of loneliness. When the words of the deficiency stories like 'I'm a loser' and 'I'm an idiot' and 'I'm dumb' dissolved I came to the body and felt what I had been running from all along. I felt all those sensations that were attached to me many times in my life when I felt unwanted by my friends, not good enough and alone. When I first felt the sensations, they felt hard. I didn't want to feel them. I started using the techniques; I found the edges of the sensations and felt the space where there was no emotion and no charge. I darted between the space and the sensations. I started dipping my toes in to feel the edges of the sensations. I 'looked' at the sensations in momentary glances and had a big, long break in the space where I could rest, feel safe and regulate my nervous system.

The more I stayed, allowed, and welcomed the sensations they started losing their ferocity, charge and power. It was more manageable, and it felt okay to be with. Then, like so many times, sensations that were so painful morphed and transformed before my eyes into the most blissful experience, and my whole body was filled with ultimate, expansive peace. Just as my depression was my medicine, so was my loneliness.

I came home to myself. I felt like I had discovered and re-found everything I had always been looking for: acceptance, approval, love and friendship from my friends. Yet all that time, I was missing myself as my own best friend! It was like my most perfect fit for a friend was there all along. But I didn't see her. I was blind to myself. I was the one I had been looking for. Opening myself up to feeling everything that came with feeling lonely was like putting parts and pieces of myself back together into one whole again. I felt complete. Any need for anything external fell away.

Since then, particular friendships and relationships have changed. I often felt an underlying neediness and dissatisfaction where I was never quite receiving what I needed from my friendships. I felt needy. I didn't want to look needy, so I didn't ask for much, if anything. But I longed for more support and more love from my friends. And I often left outings with some friends feeling undernourished or incomplete. Now, I feel a sense of satisfaction to be with myself, stay with myself, nurture the parts that feel triggered and support myself by placing my direct attention on the sensations in my body. From that place of wholeness from within, I can connect with others with authenticity, without needing so much from them, because I am already full.

Crying With Pleasure

When you feel the urge, do you let yourself cry?

A recent study by Australia Talks on the number of times people cry shows some interesting results:

- 19% of men reported they have never cried
- 31% of men reported they cried once per year
- 34% of women reported they cried once a month
- 14% of women reported they cried once per week [26]

When these results were released, Associate Professor Simon Rice from the Centre for Youth Mental Health at Melbourne University highlighted there are strong messages in our culture that crying is a sign of weakness, crying implies a sense of vulnerability, and that boys and men are encouraged to cope in different ways due to a sense of shame and embarrassment. While the suicide rates in men are three times higher.

As a woman who grew up feeling silly for needing to cry often, I can acknowledge the shame and embarrassment females feel too. I see women trying to hide their tears, distracting themselves by stating, "anyway" to shift the conversation to something lighter and more positive, or self-deprecating with words such as "I don't know why I'm so upset". Crying is not so welcome in our society.

However, it holds so much healing, beauty and relief for our bodies and minds. Crying produces oxytocin – the feel-good hormone – it activates the rest and digest response and helps us return to a state of emotional equilibrium and calm. Being held in a safe space in a KI session and being encouraged by my KI Facilitators to stay with the sensations that came with crying, had me fall in love with the act of crying. Crying transformed from being something to be afraid and ashamed of to something that brought me deep pleasure.

One of my clients, Jim, told me after his first two sessions with me, he caught himself in the act of stopping his urge to cry. He checked-in to the feeling and realised his tears were not tears of sadness but absolute joy. He was baffled by his automatic response to shut down something that felt so pleasurable. So he proceeded to let himself cry and felt the full joy of it.

When you cry, have you noticed how it feels to have emotion rise through your body? Normally, when we cry, we are in the pain of the story or we are feeling shame about crying. Now I cry very differently. I notice how the sensations in my body feel as I cry. Often there is sensation in my chest, my throat or my abdomen. Sometimes there is heat in my face as tears fall down my cheeks. It's fascinating to 'watch' how it feels in my own internal landscape when I cry. This stops me from feeling like I'm falling apart when I cry, and I get to fully embrace and love the sensations that come with crying.

Chapters Five and Six have shown you the first steps to process your thoughts and emotions using Simple Inquiry, compassionate awareness and acceptance. This is a prerequisite for diving deeper to clearing the bigger baggage that is linked to significant memories and deficiency stories.

Are you ready to clear your pain from the roots? Then let's dive into Chapter Seven together.

CHAPTER SEVEN
Clearing The Roots

Anything you avoid in life will come back, over and over again, until you're willing to face it—to look deeply into its true nature.
- Adyashanti

So far, we've explored how we automatically and unconsciously create deficiency stories about ourselves and the world through traumatic and distressing experiences. We have investigated how the body's nervous system rewires itself for protection. You've been guided through the simple steps to befriend your thoughts and process your emotions using Simple Inquiry. Now I'm going to show you how to dive deeper to heal core wounds and process painful memories and distressing experiences. If you're feeling nervous, your nerves are completely welcome and safe in this space. Remember, you can choose to try the techniques or just watch from the sidelines.

To heal my depression, I had to go beyond basic mindfulness and meditation. I had to be willing to go to the depths of what was driving my pain and sadness. Staying with basic mindfulness and meditation simply wasn't enough. A fifteen-year-old client of mine shared my realisation. She once told her Mum, "there's only so much breathing I can do". Taking deep breaths is great to regulate your nervous system when you're panicked or angry but not enough to take the deep pain of being deficient away.

What dissolved that lurking mess under my bonnet was going towards it. Safely. I learned how to face the things that had me in fear. This included my fear of my depression. I learned how to let myself be as droopy, sad and heavy as my body craved. Moving beyond the threshold brought me to feel a deep sense of wholeness, like I came home to myself.

Last year, I went to a funeral for a young woman named Holly, local to me, who suicided at 21. She was the daughter of my midwife who had helped me birth my daughter, Maggie, at home. I could relate very well to Holly's story. I was in my early twenties when I was at rock-bottom. Within her eulogy, her dad spoke of her ability to inspire others and her love of having fun and to party. He also shared that when she was home alone, the voices in her head became too much. I experienced this rollercoaster too.

After becoming a Certified Kiloby Inquiries Facilitator, I coined a new term to describe how the Kiloby Inquiries is different to basic mindfulness. I refer to the techniques as a form of Applied Mindfulness. Applied Mindfulness is the process of applying mindfulness to triggers, distressing experiences and painful memories so the root cause of our stress, depression, anxiety and pain dissolves and falls away.

With Applied Mindfulness, we're not putting out spot fires. We're finding the culprit that keeps lighting them. And the 'culprit' ends up being a friend, a golden gift, our teacher, our guide with the most beautiful messages and purpose for being here. This monstrous culprit that we ridicule is the part of ourselves that has us arrive at deep peace and immense freedom.

Earlier on, I shared that when I heard the words in my head 'I'm falling apart', it would send me into a spiralling mess. On a difficult day in 2019, I expressed these words to a mentor. She replied with "Are you really falling apart?". Her question stopped me in my tracks. What does she mean? I was stunned and confused. I do fall apart. I've always fallen apart. I had never questioned whether I was falling apart or not.

Deep down, a part of me felt like she was taking away something that I wanted to keep. I wanted to hold onto 'falling apart'. And at the same time, I looked at myself in a fresh light and thought, *well, I'm not really falling apart.*

What does 'falling apart' mean? I'm crying and I'm sad but is my body breaking down? No. Am I losing my mind? No. It's still here. I'm still functioning and parenting and getting out of bed and doing all the things a thirty-six-year-old mum, wife and sole trader does. This was the start of the end of my depression.

When we can compartmentalise our pain and depression it feels safer to tend to our deepest wounds. Each time we stay with, accept, love and nurture every part of our pain and depression, we heal it. The heaviness leaves the body. And we feel lighter.

A gentle reminder, healing our deepest wounds takes patience.

Strike up a conversation with your feelings

When you can feel sensations in your body that feel stuck, remember they are your greatest teachers. Imagine you are sitting with them in a sacred space, and you feel humbled to be in their presence. Open a conversation between you and these sensations. Ask the sensation what it wants. Ask it what it needs. See if you can give the sensation what it needs or wants. This helps to reveal the deficiency stories, emotions and painful memories that are keeping the sensations stuck. Then the sensations can process and clear. For a full list of questions to ask your feelings, watch my video on Mining using this QR code:

Go to the worst-case scenario

Clearing our pain from the root involves going towards what we fear most. A poignant question to ask is: 'What's the worst that could happen?' This is a question we rarely dare to answer. We don't want to go there. We don't want to frighten ourselves and have us spiral into some horrible negativity that we can't muster ourselves out of. We don't want to end up in a panic attack. We're trying to be calm, resilient, focused.

But when we don't consider the worst-case scenario, we spend the rest of our lives running from the idea of the worst-case scenario. We try to stay positive. Visualise the best-case scenario. Set intentions. Repeat mantras and positive affirmations. But when I ask this question and look at all of the words, pictures and body sensations that come through my answers, going to the worst-case scenario sets me free.

The first time a KI Facilitator asked me this, I felt a huge weight lifted from my shoulders. Since I was a child, I felt I was here on Earth for an important mission. To fulfill a purpose and save the world in one way or another. Coupled with this feeling, I felt immense pressure to fulfill this purpose. If I didn't, it would mean I had failed the mission.

My KI Facilitator asked me what would happen if I failed? My answer was that I wouldn't fulfill my purpose. I was prompted again. "What if you don't fulfill your purpose?" My answer intuitively rose to the surface, "I will have to come back in my next life and do it again." We inquired further. "And what's the worst thing about having to come back and do it again?" And it hit me. So what? I shrugged. It didn't matter.

All that time I had been stressed out about fulfilling my purpose and frantically striving, doing and achieving to make sure I didn't fail my mission. Until I realised there was no problem if it didn't happen. I felt such relief. The weight of saving the world had been lifted from my shoulders. Simply by asking 'what's the worst that could happen?'

Weave the techniques

Multiple questions can be woven together to process pain and reduce the intensity of our thoughts. Recently, I was preparing a program for secondary students to learn the techniques that dissolved my depression. I don't want them to have to suffer for as long as so many of us have. As I worked on the program, I felt big fears arise. When I asked myself, "What's the worst that could happen?" My answer was, "they would laugh at me and make jokes about me." I continued my Inquiry by asking myself, "if they laugh at me and make jokes about me, what does that mean about me?" The answer that came automatically was, "I'm an idiot." Bang. That's the deficiency story.

But wait. We can go deeper. You can ask yourself: 'when was the first time you felt like…' and finish the question with your deficiency story. I asked myself, 'When was the first time you felt like an idiot?' Immediately, my memory of netball training arose. It was the painful picture I held in my mind with that one team member. She had the white ball in her hands. The gym was brightly-lit. She was laughing with our team mates about me, *right in front of me*. "All she needs is glasses", she scoffed. It was the external evidence that confirmed my internal story. I *was* an idiot and a loser.

So, to process this suppressed pain, I looked at this picture with the words, 'all she needs is glasses', 'loser' and 'idiot'. I watched those words from a place of love, acceptance and gentleness. From an objective viewpoint, as if I was watching a movie. I looked at the space around the words and pictures until those words and pictures dissolved. I took a deep breath and then came to the body to feel.

Deep-seated deficiency stories and painful memories like these can surface again and again. It can take time for these words and pictures to process. But the more we welcome them and look at them, the more they lose their charge and power. Words like 'idiot' and 'loser' used to feel like a stab in the gut. But after looking at these words from a place of gentle awareness many times, they don't mean so much to me anymore. They are not who I am. They are merely words. If the same words and pictures continue to resurface for you, you're not failing. Keep welcoming them. They are your path to healing.

Even now, I still have words and pictures to look at. On difficult days, I still have people in my life that when I am in their company, my head is screaming with deficiency. And these are the parts to love. Life is simply giving us moments to love even more parts of ourselves.

In today's world of instant gratification, we expect to process our big feelings quickly and efficiently. But the truth is, we have suppressed a lot for a long time. It takes *time* to process the feelings we felt at the crucial moments in our lives. An insightful question to ask here is: 'what if I have to process my feelings forever?'. Put the words of your answer on the screen and look at them with love before feeling the feelings. Healing from the inside out is not a one-pill-a-day-situation. It's a lifetime of feeling the feelings we didn't feel.

I felt angry and blamed others for not showing me how to feel my feelings. Why didn't anyone tell me to sit down and feel my feelings? Why didn't anyone show me that emotions are not something to fear? Why didn't anyone show me how my body can process its own emotions? If they showed me what seems so simple now, I wouldn't have been stuck in the pain of depression for so many years.

But I look at people around me and realise they are not aware of their own feelings. Many can't sit still; they have to be doing something. Many people couldn't stand doing nothing. You might hear people say, "I have to be busy, that is who I am." Is it who we are? Or have we lost the capacity to be with ourselves? Have we lost the ability to stay with ourselves, be connected with ourselves and have a relationship with ourselves?

Many people are not living in their bodies. They are not feeling their feelings. They are not allowing full waves of tears to come through their bodies. Many have not experienced the value of curiously watching the sensations in the body that come with crying. Many people are in their heads, *all the time*, like I was. It's easy to dismiss the impact of emotions when it comes to mental health because most are not aware of their own emotions. I believe no one showed me how to feel my feelings because no one around me knew how.

Many are not aware, or won't admit, they have a subconscious mind filled with even fleeting, negative stories about themselves; that deep down there is a part of them that believes they are hopeless, unloveable, weak, a failure, not worth it, not good enough. And when they do realise, they might refocus on a positive thought or keep it hidden out of shame. Open and authentic sharing about this innate part of being human can be difficult to find.

People who are sensitive, feel more than those who are not sensitive. Their joy is more intense and so is their pain. Being resilient, bouncing back and shifting their attention from a negative to a positive is difficult and, at times, impossible. There is a plethora of guidance to be more positive through cognitive behaviour therapy, growth mindset and positive psychology. But focusing on the positives is unattainable for people who are sensitive and carrying a heavy load of emotional baggage. The only way to clear the negativity is to *go* to the negativity.

Identify what your negativity is made of

Let's explore what your negativity is made of. What words arise for you when you think of your own negativity? What sensations arise in your body? Are there pictures of people, worst-case scenarios in your head about what could happen in the future? Or are there horrible, negative memories you don't want to look at? Whatever your negative mess looks like, everything can be boiled down to words, pictures and body sensations. List the words that come with your negativity. Take those words to Simple Inquiry. And add the pictures that go with those words. Then come to the body and feel.

Negativity is often a picture in the mind that is stuck to sensations. It might be like a scary monster looming in the background or a bad energy on your shoulder. But when you look at what makes up the scary picture, all you will find is words, pictures and body sensations. You might have felt so terrified of being overpowered by your negativity or exhausted from trying to escape it, but looking at the words, pictures and body sensations that make up negativity has it slink away into nothing. If you feel more of a sense of a scary monster or bad energy, don't fall for that trick! You can look at the words 'sense, scary monster, bad energy' or come to the body to feel it directly.

When I teach this approach to parents of children who are struggling with their mental health, they feel like they are finally getting the answers they've been desperately seeking. After being introduced to the Kiloby Inquiries for her child, one Mum shared, "I totally resonated with your talk and gained further insight into how words, pictures and feelings are so interconnected and the importance of looking at them objectively... a huge piece of information. I can now see why the professional psychology help offered now needs to radically change." This new science and these new techniques bring a sigh of relief for so many.

Learning how to process the negatives brought me peace at work. Active on social media for my business, I had fears about what certain people would think of me when I imagined them reading my posts. I found my shoulders would tense up and I wanted to escape myself. I was full of shame. I felt ugly and cringed at myself in embarrassment. I thought they were thinking I was an idiot. Annoying. Self-obsessed. An ego-maniac. I used to push through the negativity to feel more positive and better about myself. I used positive affirmations and high-vibing visualisations. But the body never lies.

When we shift our vibration into a higher state of consciousness without going to the root of our own discomfort, we are slowing our growth and evolution and delaying the inevitable. It's like we are dragging all of our luggage, all of the muck we have accumulated over the years onto the plane for our next big adventure and wondering why we don't feel light, free and breezy. This whole mess that we want to escape can be simply broken down into words, pictures and body sensations. And with our tender attention on them, the root of the problem clears.

Use Reverse Inquiry

You might question how we know that the root of the problem has been cleared. We want to check that we have integrated every piece of discomfort and pain associated with the story that has arisen. Otherwise, the emotional memory remains stored in the body to manifest into mental illness and according to modern science, physical disease. We use a technique called Reverse Inquiry to check the body is clear. You can watch me explain Reverse Inquiry using this QR code:

Let's imagine you feel like a bad person. Maybe you've made a mistake at work that's cost your colleague precious time. You might think, 'He must hate me. I'm hopeless. My boss is going to kill me when he finds out.' Perhaps you've asked yourself, 'what does this mean about me that I've made a mistake?' And your answer is: 'I'm a bad employee'. You may have dived deeper and asked yourself, 'when was the first time I felt like a bad employee', and a memory of you making mistakes as a fifteen-year-old shop assistant surfaces.

As part of an influx of thoughts, you might remember a time when you were four. Your grandma was yelling at you for leaving the soap in the bath. The words 'bad girl' or 'naughty girl' arise. You look at the words, pictures and body sensations that come with this whole scenario until the body feels clear. Then you check that there's nothing else to clear from the body using Reverse Inquiry.

To use the Reverse Inquiry verbally state the opposite of what your deficiency story is. In this case, the core deficiency story is 'I'm bad', so you verbalise "I'm *not* bad". As you say these words, watch to see if your body and mind agrees, disagrees, or is neutral about it.

If your body agrees, you might have a nice, warm, inspired, pleasant, excited or peaceful feeling come through your body as it hears your words. If it's neutral about your statement, you won't feel any reaction at all in the body. If the body disagrees, you will definitely feel a sensation in the body. This might be anything from a slight flutter in the gut to a strong surge of tension rising through your head, chest and throat.

If your mind agrees, it might naturally say something like 'Yes, I'm not bad'. If it disagrees, it might rebut with a remark such as 'That's not true' and raise other memories of when you have felt like a bad person. Look at all of these words and pictures to process them before coming to the body to feel all the feelings. Otherwise, if your mind neither agrees nor disagrees, rest in the stillness.

If the body or mind disagreed, and you've sat with the words, pictures and body sensations verbalise the same statement again to check your reaction. Each time you verbalise the statement and process the thoughts and feelings, the body's response reduces. Once your body and mind have no aversion to the statement, you have cleared your emotional memory of the deficiency story.

Now, it may come up again during another scenario, or the next time you make a mistake but the more you turn towards the words, pictures and body sensations that arise when you are triggered, the less threatening they become, and the less you identify with the deficiency story. Generally, you feel clearer, lighter and you process thoughts and feelings more easily. Keep looking at them as they arise. Celebrate that they are here to be welcomed and loved. Then they will clear.

If your body disagrees, it is easy to feel like you've failed. But you haven't. In fact, it's a celebration! Every time you are aware of more words and pictures and go towards them with love, you are one step closer to clearing them from your body and mind.

Journaling can be a beautiful way to become more aware of your deficiency stories and negative sense of self that has been driving your life.

List your deficiency stories. Consider what might be your core deficiency stories. What are the events in your life or the memories that had you arrive at these deficiency stories? Draw your web of stories on the outline of a tree. Write your core deficiency stories on the root of the tree and your deficiency stories on the branches. Have your surface-level problems like money worries, career indecision and relationship hurdles on the leaves of the trees. Then take one story or one memory that holds a strong charge to Simple Inquiry.

Sometimes the root of our pain can surface as social anxiety. Imagine you're freaking out because you've seen *that* person again and you always tense up around them. You wish you could be *normal*, relaxed and yourself when you're in their company. But when you're around them, your throat might constrict, maybe you freeze, and you find it hard to talk.

When I was in that situation, I would always be wondering what was wrong with me, why couldn't I be normal like everyone else? And why was I so weird? Now I know that this is the body's automatic response to protect itself from a threat. My body is so intelligent that it picks up signals from my external environment to scan and check if it's safe. In this case, the other person is a perceived threat. To ensure my safety, I adopt a defensive persona (fight response), I try to avoid eye contact (flight response), I don't know what to say (freeze response) or I people-please (please response). My responses are not weird, they are automatic and serve me.

Rather than trying to pull away from the discomfort of this situation, I put my x-ray-like vision on the sensations in the body. I say things like 'oh, isn't that interesting that there are sensations in my throat'. I find the perimeter of the sensation and notice the space it. Rather than wishing the awkward discomfort would fly away, I play with the idea that it is safe to have these sensations here in my body. A warmth comes around me as I hold both the warm, gentle, compassionate space around me and have the sensation there. This helps me feel safe.

When we lose the need for the sensation to leave, we welcome, love and accept ourselves just as we are, *including* the sensations. The sensations are a part of us. When we allow the sensations to be in the body, we can feel safe in our skin. There is nothing from which to escape. They are just sensations. They are feelings; things you can *feel* in the body. When we welcome them, there is no problem.

The biggest thing I learnt the year I dissolved my depression was that there was nothing wrong with me. All those years, I was searching for the answer to fix me, to solve my problem, to stop crying, to have more confidence, to stop having to take anti-depressants, to stop the horrible stories in my head. I felt like I'd searched high and low, and had been at my wits end in my own head trying to find something that worked so I wasn't depressed anymore.

In the middle of 2019, when I was practising KI in a one-on-one session, the penny dropped. All humans have thoughts and feelings. We have rising sensations in the body. We have thoughts that come and go. It's normal to experience thoughts and feelings.

I realised there was nothing wrong with me. There never was anything wrong with me. I'm not broken. There's nothing to fix. I'm okay and enough just as I am. Arriving at this knowing, of understanding this in my bones, my blood, and in my body ushered in a flood of tears of relief. I simply hadn't been shown how to feel safe with my thoughts and feelings. Once I was shown how to feel safe with them, I stopped getting sucked into believing the stories, and my feelings lost their fear factor. Then I was free.

When you reach for the root of your problems, you will find yourself at the same core deficiency stories time and again. Your deficiency stories will not be dissimilar to mine. We humans hold the same stories. I asked over 700 people who practise the Kiloby Inquiries what their core deficiency stories were and their answers were all very common! We are all walking around with similar versions of the same stories of ourselves. We pretend that we don't hold these stories or are unaware that these stories are driving our whole personality.

We are in a place of protection more than we think. We are terrified of being seen, being heard, being hurt, being told off, so we keep our thoughts and feelings hidden. We feel shame to be holding these deficiency stories because a part of us believes them to be true. We build our identity into something that we perceive to be more positive and socially acceptable. Breaking the taboo about negative thoughts will help us come out of hiding and feel safe to be with the vulnerable parts of ourselves and each other.

When we feel safe, we don't resist what sensations are in the body. We know we are safe with any sensations in our bodies, whether we are on our own, on stage, with one person, with a group, doing what we love or doing what we don't particularly like. When we hand our bodies over to the sensations, we are free.

Surrendering to our sensations does not mean to hand our power over in relationships with other people. Creating boundaries in our connection with others is healthy, important and an act of self-love. We are the creator and the driver of our own lives and get to choose what intentions, words and decisions feel right for ourselves. We are also our own sacred steward who protects the body. We stand up and say no when we need to.

But when we are communing with ourselves, and returning to peace and freedom, we can relax within the boundaries of our sacred space. Our bodies. Play with opening your body like a big ocean and have the sensations run effortlessly and freely throughout it. Notice how your heart might open and offer warmth as you feel safe in your own skin. Once you feel safe within your own body, you can feel safe with other people. When you realise you're not the deficiency stories, you can relate with others with an open heart. You can feel compassion for them and forgive them for the words they've said or not said.

Understanding the root of others' hurtful behaviour can help you let go of the past. You can give up the fight of being right or wrong and realise hurt people hurt people. Hurt people behave from a negative and mentally constructed sense of self. When we hold space for ourselves – our negative sense of self *and* loving hearts – we can stop fighting and surrender into feeling safe and free.

Part of feeling free is building the capacity to cry. When I have the urge to cry, I have a strong wave of sensations rise from my gut to my throat. My heart can feel heavy. The thoughts that often arise for me are: 'is it appropriate to cry right now?' and 'what will they think if I cry?'

Then I remember it's okay to cry. At times, I put my head in my hands and let the sensations rise through my heart and into my throat and jaw. If I'm in company, I hope they don't disrupt my release with well-meaning remarks to save me. I am deeply grateful when I'm given the space to cry. I feel deep relief and full body pleasure. Then the release. It's perfect to cry.

What if everyone is craving to cry? What if we are all wanting permission to cry rather than putting on a brave face, soldiering on? What if my crying opens the space for the next person to feel free to cry? Whenever she wants. Wherever he wants. With whomever they want. Just imagine the global healing and release that could occur. Rather than walking around like pressure cookers. We could just cry!

Do you feel resistance to cry? What do you think it means about you when you cry? That you're weak, hopeless, a loser or a burden? Whatever your answer, that's the deficiency story blocking you from the pleasurable freedom that can come with crying. Take those words to Simple Inquiry and then feel the sensations. Keep practising every time you hear or feel resistance. Eventually your resistance will clear, and you will be free to be human.

Explore how you're benefiting from the worst

Upon my healing journey towards recovery from mental illness, I was shocked to realise I had been benefiting from having depression. For many years, all I could see was that I was sad, crying, and negative all the time. I wished I was different. But I was blind to the fact that I was gaining something from being depressed. Using a special technique called the Utility Inquiry brought all of that out into the open and helped me see I was clinging to my depression.

You can watch me explain the Utility Inquiry using this QR code:

Using the Utility Inquiry, I asked myself what I got out of having depression. My answer shocked me. I got love. I instantly thought of my husband, Leigh. I saw us sitting on the couch with him comforting me, giving me love and adoring attention and helping me through my mental battles. I explored further by asking, 'what if my depression went away?' My answer was cutting – I will be left alone. I realised in that moment that I had subconsciously been wanting to stay depressed as a way of ensuring I was being fed the love and attention I needed. If I stopped being depressed, I feared Leigh's loving attention would disappear and I would be alone.

There doesn't need to be shame around these behaviours. Clinging to something like depression was a coping mechanism to help me feel safe. We naturally behave in certain ways to receive the love we crave.

Babies cry when they are not picked up to ensure they are held, comforted, soothed, loved and receive their needs. Children demonstrate attention-seeking behaviour when they feel unsafe within themselves and need love and attention. Holding onto mental illness can offer us safety and protection.

You can explore whether part of you is holding onto mental illness. Maybe it is serving you, helping you, protecting you in some way.

Ask yourself what you get out of having depression or anxiety. Wait for the intuitive response to rise to the surface. Maybe it keeps people close to you so you're not alone or it keeps you small, contained and safe from being hurt or disappointed.

Try it a different way.

Verbally say, "I get nothing out of having depression". Then immediately watch how your body and mind respond. Do they agree or disagree? Did your body flare up with sensations? Is there a pulling in your stomach or a flutter through your heart? Whatever sensations arose, stay and feel them as they express themselves for as long as they need. Did your mind chime in with a rebuttal? Investigate further and ask, 'what do I get out of having depression?' Then take your answer to Simple Inquiry.

When a deficiency story keeps popping up time and again or if a sensation won't leave the body, ask how you are benefiting from it. What is it giving you? How are you gaining from this story or sensation? Is it protecting you? Remember your body and mind are not the enemy; they are working for you. They are helping and serving you. Thank them for helping you by wrapping your arms around you. Love yourself, just as you are.

When I reflect on my early-twenties, my binge-eating was a method of escaping my loneliness and sense of deficiency. I was too afraid to reach out to particular friends in case I looked too desperate. So I sat at home and compulsively ate biscuits, bread, chocolate, nuts and lollies. Deep in shame, I ensured I never ate too much so I could keep my eating disorder hidden from my family.

I couldn't stop eating. At work, I would eat two lunches even though I wasn't hungry. I ate food I didn't even want or like. I ate until I was so full, and my jaw hurt from chewing. My compulsive behaviour instilled a fear that there was something wrong with me.

I hated food. I wished I didn't have to think about eating. Then I wouldn't have to worry about eating too much. In my early-twenties while at university, I had gained fifteen kilograms on top of my normal weight. I felt ashamed to eat in front of others, which left me starving at work. After work, I would chow down blocks of chocolate and giant chocolate chip cookies. This left me with no appetite for dinner, and I would head to bed in self-hatred and self-disgust that I had done it *again*.

Fifteen years later, my addiction moved from sugar to scrolling on social media. One day, I was shocked to see my phone usage had crept up to five hours a day, mostly on Facebook. I was scrolling my way through the day, trying to numb the frustration, anger, discomfort and pain of motherhood.

I love my kids. They are the most beautiful children in the whole world. I love playing with them and watching them engrossed in their drawings. I love holding their hands as we walk through the bush together and I love listening to their stories. But when the three of them are demanding my attention for more things, more help, more food, more play, more drinks, staying present with their needs and feelings, as well as my own can be confronting.

When life is confronting, I am stuck in Velcro. I want to escape. The quickest relief I was finding was in the endless burst of fresh posts on Facebook. I was self-medicating with my phone. I was numbing the sensations in my body so I couldn't feel. I escaped through my phone just as I had escaped through food.

Learning how to turn inward and feel safe with my rising emotions eased my reliance on social media. Curiously going towards my feelings took my need for them to go away. I learnt how to be with myself rather than be with my phone.

If I'm not mindful, my phone usage still increases without me noticing. I find the more I use it, the more I need it. But when I prioritise being with myself, I feel more comfortable in my own company and don't need a distraction.

When I am aware and connected with myself, I am quite content to sit alone without doing anything. I can sit on my bed and look at the wall with my words and pictures until they fall away and then take my attention to my body and feel. This simple act of being with myself is deeply satisfying, nourishing and pleasurable.

From this space of awareness, I don't need anything outside of myself. I am fully resourced and whole. I feel a lot of spaciousness around me and a deep sense of peace within. I get a sense that nothing needs doing and I have all the time in the world to simply be. This deep sense of clarity, connection and satisfaction is a far cry from the stressed, overworking perfectionist I was for many years.

After pushing myself to burn-out, striving for my next big goal, I realised I didn't have to achieve anything. I realised my pushing and over-achieving was driven by not feeling good enough. So I rested for many months. After about six months of rest, I gradually returned to my creations.

From there, for the most part, I have created from a different place. Not from a place of needing to be someone special or to fix the world of its disarray. But from a place of joyful self expression, injecting things that will help and support the world in its divinely perfect form. I realised I didn't need fixing and neither did the world.

This has been a deep-dive to reveal the hidden stories and memories that can attach to the body and bind the nervous system into an ongoing state of survival. I want to celebrate you for journeying deeply. Now we can come up for air! The next chapter shows you how to hold space for yourself and hold space for others. This is the key to creating a new world where we can leave our protective shell of pain and return to the beauty of connection with those around us.

CHAPTER EIGHT
Holding Space

Opinion is really the lowest form of human knowledge. It requires no accountability, no understanding. The highest form of knowledge is empathy, for it requires us to suspend our egos and live in another's world. It requires profound purpose larger than the self kind of understanding.

- Plato

In the midst of depression, speaking my needs felt impossible. I remember as a teenager, my sister Erin was almost pleading with me to speak so she could listen and help. As I've shared with you, I desperately wanted to talk. But a loud, repetitive voice in my mind told me I was selfish if I talked about myself and my problems. In this case, 'I am selfish' was the deficiency story. So I stayed silent and cried alone.

It took years for Mum to learn to keep prodding me to speak. She would keep asking 'What is wrong'... 'and what else is wrong?' ... 'and what else is wrong?' Then she would finish with 'are you sure there's nothing else?' and 'you're absolutely sure?' Over time, I would slowly bleed out dribs and drabs. I was so thankful she stayed in the conversation with me as I fought the nasty voice inside my mind.

It's our deficiency stories that keep us from sharing our worries. We are frightened of speaking for fear of being rejected or ridiculed. We feel vulnerable with our hearts open, so we stay silent to protect ourselves. This is why it helps to have people in your life who know how to hold space for you. When we feel safe in another's company, we start to open up and find relief in that connection.

Most people want to try and help with their well-meaning advice but advice can do more damage. My constant internal pressure to do better and be better was exacerbated when I was told by others to do more of this and be more of that. Our societal obsession with staying positive, upbeat and full of energy can leave people with depression feeling wrong for feeling down, tired and negative.

When I had the courage to share how I was really feeling, at times I felt slammed with advice. For every practical, positive solution someone gave me, the more inadequate I felt. I was overwhelmed by all the things others thought I should be doing and felt like more of a hopeless case than before.

Deep or active listening is hard. Even though I know how unhelpful advice was for me when I was depressed, I still find myself in my own battle to keep my mouth shut when I am absolutely bursting to add my two cents worth. In my mind, I can see the problem and I know how to fix it. My left-brain is dominant, and I can see a practical, logical and sequential solution to the problem. But I'm not meeting the person where they are at. I'm not holding space for that person to arrive at their own answers.

When I wanted to vent about how terrible life was, I didn't want answers. I wanted to vent. I wanted to express myself. I didn't want a solution. I simply wanted my feelings validated. I wanted acknowledgement that life was hard and that it was okay to be struggling. I just wanted to be seen and loved.

Holding Space For Others

If you know someone with depression or anxiety, holding space can be the most compassionate act and a lifeline for them. It is like holding a safe space for someone to be loved, appreciated, cared for and supported. In this space, the person is welcome as they are. Holding space is like holding the person in a beautiful, warm and safe cocoon where they can simply be themselves.

Imagine you have two massive imaginary arms around the person you are holding space for, holding the energy or 'space' around their body. These two arms hold them with love in a way that they can relax. In this space they don't have to change any part of themselves. They are accepted and loved just the way they are.

You are offering protection and holding safe boundaries for that person to show up as they are. You create a compassionate space for that person to express what's happening for them without your judgment. Gradually, they feel safe enough to take off their protective masks and be authentically themselves. They don't have to hide their emotions. Crying is welcome. You compassionately offer stillness and listen as they share, cry, yell, scream, sob, overtalk, talk rationally, talk irrationally, and everything else in between. You are there for them.

When holding space for someone, you tend to talk less than the person you're holding space for. You're offering sounds like "mmm" so the person feels encouraged to speak and gets what they need off their chest. You're practising deep listening, reflective listening, and you're offering prompts like "tell me more", to help them know they are wanted and loved.

The simple act of holding space is often missed because we are unconsciously tuned to our often judgmental internal dialogue. Your own internal dialogue could include your opinion about the situation, judgment on whether the person is taking the right approach or not, or a compulsion to fix their problem for them. When listening to someone in their struggle, we are often waiting for them to pause, so we can say what we want to say. And if we don't say what we want to say, we can feel pent up, exasperated or like we are going to explode.

This is the Velcro Effect, in action. The words could be 'if only they followed my advice' and the sensations might be heat in your face, agitation in your shoulders and pressure in your chest. In this case, as the listener, your deficiency stories are being triggered.

The most important part of holding space is deep listening. Deep listening is where you are actively engaged in receiving everything the person is telling you with empathy and understanding. The magic of listening is when the person feels accepted as they are, welcome to be themselves, and like they belong. What a gift this is to give someone.

Stillness can be a gift in conversation. It gives the other person an opportunity to share, to be heard and to feel received, loved and valued. It is not about gluing your mouth shut and denying your own expression. It is about being radically present with the other person and their needs. Your stillness is the doorway to their own self-empowerment.

Recently, I had my two eldest children, Jackson and Ivy upset on the couch with me. While I cuddled them, I practised being quiet and refraining from saying things to make them feel better. I responded to their worries with soothing sounds like "mmm" and empathised with them with a simple "yeah". After a couple of minutes they had processed their feelings and co-regulated their nervous systems with mine. And that was that.

Next time you are having a conversation with someone, notice how much of the time you are listening to what the other person is saying. And notice how much you are listening to your own internal dialogue. Start to play with the idea of not saying what you want to say, and instead, notice the sensations in your body, hear the other person, nod and give verbal cues that invite them to talk.

Learning how to hold space for others is work in progress. Despite practising holding space in both my personal and professional life for close to twenty years, I still find myself jumping in to fix their problems. I try to make the other person better and forget to listen.

Our need to try to fix others rubs off on our children early. When Ivy was four, she was upset that we took her training wheels off her bike. At aged six, Jackson was building with frustration because nothing he was doing was making her feel better. I told him it wasn't our job to make her happy, it was our job to stay with her while she was sad. We spent a few minutes cuddling her and stroking her hair before she was laughing again.

Well-meaning advice can be swapped out for acknowledging the other person and practising reflective listening. Reflective listening is the process of reflecting back what you have heard. You might say "I am hearing you are having a really hard time", or "If I was in your shoes, I would feel angry too". Empathy goes a long way.

If you are finding it challenging to listen without giving advice, here are some journal prompts or questions to ponder:

- what does it mean about me that they are unhappy or depressed?
- what if that person never gets over their problem?
- what would it mean about me if I couldn't fix that person's problem?
- what's the worst thing that could happen if I listened to that person without giving advice?

Then take your answers to Simple Inquiry so you can process what is yours.

When I am not consciously listening to the person and just giving advice, I am in my head, I am not grounded, and my heart is closed. We live in a world where grounding and opening the heart is often considered crazy, so I will try to put this simply.

Being grounded with your heart open is a precursor for holding space, listening, and deep connection with yourself and another person.

Being grounded can be just as an elusive concept as 'holding space' and 'opening your heart'. If you're stuck in your head, you might be like, 'what is that? I don't get it'. Or you might palm it off as something airy-fairy and woo-woo. The rational mind and left-brain loves logic, sequence, facts and practicalities. But the rational mind is not all that we are. We have the right hemisphere of the brain, our bodies, a heart, and a bio-field that reaches far beyond our physical bodies.

The more grounded and embodied you are, the less you are stuck in your head and its conveyor belt of thoughts, and the more present, relaxed and open you are to listening to yourself and the people around you.

When you ground your body, your attention comes from being in the mind to be embodied. You are living in your body. Being embodied means you are aware of the physical sensations in your body as you go about your day. The more moments you practise being in your body every day, the more peace, freedom, beauty and pleasure you will feel. When I am grounded, I feel deeply connected with myself. I am alive, present and connected with the people and the world around me. When I am deeply connected, I feel deep satisfaction with being alive.

The ground gives you stability, security, and a strong foundation. You might feel guilty to hand your worries over to Mother Earth because we humans have already inflicted so much pain on her. But she is our mother. We will always be deeply connected with her. We are not separate from the land. We are a part of nature.

When I surrender all of my worries and hand the heaviness over to the earth, I feel like I am cradled and cocooned in a warm, loving, womb-like embrace. I feel supported, nurtured, nourished and cared for. By giving all of the energy that feels dense or heavy to the ground, Mother Earth composts and transforms it into enlivened energy. I become one with her and feel supported and powerful in my endeavour, super charged with the sacred medicine of the earth.

We have a magnificent heart in the middle of our bodies. When tapped into, the heart illuminates an effortless eternal flow of love, gratitude and peace. Opening the heart brings a sense of peace, freedom and love for yourself and the person you are listening to.

Here's how to open the heart:

- ground yourself by practising natural rest or basic mindfulness

- put your attention on your heart and imagine a door opening or a flower blooming there
- notice your heart filling with a gentle, loving warmth
- see or sense this warmth spilling over the edges of your heart and flooding your body
- notice how it feels to have this warm love fill your body

Practise opening your heart before you speak to someone you want to hold space for, including yourself.

Often we think people who are depressed are draining but what if it wasn't them who was draining your energy? How would you feel if you stopped trying to make them positive? Would you feel relief if you didn't need to prop them up? What if you let them be as sad, dark and heavy as they are? Resisting others as they are, is what leaks our life force.

What if you just let them be sad? What if you just let them feel the way they do? *Ask yourself, what's the worst that could happen?* Then take your answer to Simple Inquiry. Process your own concerns and create the space for them to be negative and tired. Give them space to put words to their feelings. Let them cry their pain out.

Imagine giving them the space to arrive at their own best answers. In a busy, material world, we can forget how to access the wealth of wisdom we have within. Holding space for someone without offering advice, gives the other person an opportunity to find their own answers. Being listened to can help people believe in their own ability to trouble-shoot and problem-solve. They learn to hear their inner guidance more clearly and trust it enough to follow it.

Obviously, there are times when someone wants an answer from someone else. Perhaps their executive functioning has gone offline, they cannot think clearly, they don't know what to do and want to be guided by you. If you sense that in someone, ask them: "would you like some advice or guidance?" If they give you permission, then of course, give your advice. Your suggestions might be just what they need. But remain holding the space for them to be connected with their own source of power.

Holding Space For Yourself

If you are depressed, the reality is that people can't or don't always hold space for you. Not everyone has the capacity to listen to you without judgment. Everyone is doing their best to manage their own thoughts and emotions. We must know how to hold space for ourselves when others can't or won't.

When others can't listen, we're given an opportunity to show up for ourselves. How can we hear ourselves in the conversation? How can we let ourselves cry? How can we befriend our big feelings when others can't embrace those parts? How can we be gentle with ourselves when we are full of self-disgust, and no one seems to understand? Holding space and being responsible for ourselves in the hardest moments creates strong foundations for natural resilience.

Holding space for yourself when others don't, includes putting your attention on the sensations in your body. If you are in conversation with someone who is not listening or is giving you advice, notice how your body is responding. Welcome the body sensations, notice the space around the person and listen to the sounds of their words as if you are listening with newborn baby ears. Hold the space for all that is arising while in conversation with this person.

Holding space for yourself when you are emotionally triggered is lovingly embracing your body as your mind wants to sever it out of shame that you can't get it together or stop crying. It includes giving yourself permission to cry even when the other person is uncomfortable with your tears. Holding space for yourself includes allowing yourself to have tears run from your eyes even when someone is trying to make you stop.

When in solitude, give yourself your own hug. Wrap your own arms around you and notice how it feels. Open your heart and let the warm energy of love stream down your arms, into your hands and refill your body as you lay your hands on your skin. Be there for yourself.

Voicing our needs in conversation is important. People aren't mind readers. But knowing what our needs are, must be the first step.

Journaling can help to become clear on your needs. Set the scene with dimmed lights, beautiful music and your favourite oils or incense.

Write the question 'What do you need?' and then let yourself write, automatically. Write without any worry about what is spilling out onto the paper. Just let the words pour out on the page. You don't need to edit it.

Eventually, your writing will become clear, and it will turn into the most stunning piece of personalised guidance that is perfect for you to hear.

Once you know your needs, the next step is to verbally express them and ask for help. For many years, I didn't say how I was feeling for fear that I was asking for too much, that I was annoying and over the top. It can take real courage to put the words "I'm struggling" out in the world.

Holding Space For Yourself And Others Simultaneously

The real freedom comes when you can hold space for yourself as you hold space for others simultaneously. Everyone just wants to be acknowledged, seen, heard, and loved. We as a global community are craving it. The modern-day lifestyle with smart phones and hectic schedules can disconnect us from ourselves and each other but open-hearted connection brings peace.

Holding space for yourself and others simultaneously is a fundamental skill that strengthens authentic connection with those you love. You have needs and so do the people you're in conversation with. Your need might be to feel loved while their need might be to help.

Can you hold space for both of you and each of your needs?

Just like you would put an imaginary bubble or cocoon around you when you hold space for yourself, try including you and the other person in the space at the same time. This way, you get to be included. You get to be loved. You can meet your own needs. And the other person can feel loved and be in a space to have their needs met.

Sometimes we don't want to hold space for people who have hurt us in the past. This resistance to holding space for particular people in your life can be managed with Inquiry and guidelines. Safe boundaries or clear guidelines for what is acceptable communication is important. Aggression, including passive aggression, manipulation and mockery are not welcomed or tolerated. Safety comes first. Then you can ask, 'what's the worst that could happen if I hold space for this person?' Take your answer to Simple Inquiry.

The more we practise holding space, the better we get at it. Let's be radical and hold space for ourselves and the people around us. Let's practise listening to ourselves and each other at the same time. Let's learn how to offer love to one person at a time, one conversation at a time without any need to change their mind, change their thinking or change their actions. If you are listening to both yourself and the person in front of you, you are simply changing the world.

On my retreats and in my sacred circles, I see wild transformation in others when they are given the space to feel, express themselves and be held without severing their connection with their own emotions.

It took me time to feel comfortable with others crying. I used to squirm and feel fearful watching them cry. I wanted them to stop. But now I trust the process. Crying can feel fascinating and satiating. It's like the body cracks open. Dam walls collapse and floods of emotions that were locked inside finally feel free. After they cry, they always feel lighter and I feel honoured to witness their healing.

It takes time for others to feel safe crying. It takes time to feel comfortable crying in the company of someone else. Generally, we learn from a young age not to cry. We were told directly, or indirectly, to stop. When we fully allow ourselves to be ourselves, tears from grief to joy come and go. And when we let them come and go as they please, they don't seem to hang around.

Once my friend told me her daughter's teacher told her daughter to stop crying. Of course, this made her want to cry more. She told her teacher "I want to stop crying but I can't!" We can learn to feel shame about this natural process early.

I had a client have a memory surface when she didn't know why she was crying and her parents tried to help her stop by counting down from ten. I hear of parents asking their children to go to their room to cry or take their children aside to 'pull themselves together' when they cry. I've learnt of a mother who pays her children $50 to stop crying. It can feel difficult to manage the feelings we have about our children's feelings and fortunately the Kiloby Inquiries can help.

Imagine if we were all so comfortable with others crying in our company. We would have the freedom to cry when we needed to and when we wanted to without others around us in a flap causing a massive fuss. Just imagine how free we would feel if we could unashamedly cry at any time, and have our emotions process without being interrupted to do it somewhere more *appropriate*. We would be free to be ourselves.

CHAPTER NINE
Dreaming a New Dream

If kids can't share their anger, it doesn't cease to exist. It festers, usually causing more frequent and intense flare-ups, discharged in bursts of impulsive limit-pushing behaviour. It is also likely that unexpressed emotions like anger may be stockpiled and distilled into chronic anxiety or depression.

- Janet Lansbury

Learning from our lived experience with mental illness can help us shape a better world for the future. Through listening, we can meet the needs of those who are suffering and build mental health, educational and family systems that are more effective so we can all thrive, whether we are sensitive, carrying trauma or not.

My wish is for all people with depression and anxiety to be offered a body-based approach to improve their mental health. A set of simple techniques like the Kiloby Inquiries could make all the difference. The primary treatments I received to treat my depression was medication and talk therapy with my psychologists and counsellors. Now, having come out the other side of depression, I can see my nervous system and emotional body was neglected and needed more tailored attention and care.

In her speech at the Royal Commission for Victoria's mental health system, Penny Armytage shared, 'we must address that the mental health system is imbalanced. Under-resourcing has led to an over-reliance on medication and too little is offered by way of therapeutic and recovery-oriented services.' She went on to say, 'there is not enough focus on promotion of mental health and wellbeing despite the clear economic and social benefits.'

I dream that learning how to feel safe to feel our feelings is included in our mental health system, educational system and in our way of life. I want all mental health professionals including psychologists and counsellors to be trained in a somatic-based approach such as the Kiloby Inquiries, Somatic Experiencing, Embodied Processing or somatic counselling to support those people who don't respond to talk therapy.

Since offering Kiloby Inquiries sessions to my clients, I witness many people are terrified of going towards their pain, grief and shame. Often without knowing, I watch others innocently talk themselves out of feeling in an attempt to protect themselves from their pain. As a global community, it's time to learn how to feel safe enough to stop, rest and face the parts of us that we fear, and find our inner peace.

Throughout my treatment with many mental health professionals, I had only one psychologist who tried to guide me to the pain in my body. My resistance rose and as a result, she redirected my focus out of my body. Had she stayed with me and shown me how to process my resistance, my depression could have stopped right there.

Given somatic therapy is relatively new, she was unlikely equipped at the time to show me how to feel safe to feel and process my resistance. But with mounting evidence that supports somatic therapy, there is a wealth of professional pathways for mental health professionals to learn somatic-based techniques so they can support their clients who need it. Offering a holistic service that includes both cognitive *and* somatic-based services could save lives.

Providing techniques like the Kiloby Inquiries helps complete trauma cycles so we are not relating to ourselves, each other and the world from our own core wounds and deficiency stories. In a session, everyday problems are often linked with memories that were long forgotten. When someone can be shown safely how to return to the original trauma or wound and integrate their emotions, they can become unshackled from the past and interact in the world with an open heart.

It's vital to find a balance between engaging with positive language while learning to be present with the full spectrum of emotions. More frequent and in-depth practise to befriend negative thoughts and intense emotions using acceptance and compassion is essential for any human being, but especially for people with depression and anxiety. Learning to live with all of my emotions helped me experience a genuine, positive sense of self.

Understanding mental illness from lived experience might improve mental health campaigns in the future. During the height of the pandemic, the Head to Health[27] mental health campaign was released. The three tips to improve mental health were staying connected, keeping busy, and being active. While these tips might have been beneficial for people having a difficult day, I didn't have the capacity to practise these when I was depressed. When I was depressed, the last thing I wanted to do was to stay *connected* and see people. I certainly didn't have the energy to be *active*. And keeping busy kept me away from my own source of healing. Slowing down, being mindful, listening to our nervous system states, holding compassion for our thoughts and emotions and being aware of our own needs are the keys to thriving mental health.

Regulating and controlling emotions are terms that are misunderstood by the wider population, leaving it difficult for our children to have a healthy relationship with their own emotions.

Many of us learnt early on to squash our feelings so they were invisible. Many of our parents and teachers didn't have time to listen to our feelings. We learnt that our feelings were wrong and were a waste of time to engage with. We tossed that beautiful part of ourselves aside.

Cultural messaging can feel like we have two choices in life: feel sorry for ourselves or get on with it. We don't want to wallow, so we put on a brave face and disconnect from our emotions. Then as we look at our lives, surrounded by all the things we ever wanted, we can wonder why we don't feel so good.

Right now, resilience is a buzz word in the education world. Our children are taught at school about being resilient, being able to bounce back when they meet a challenge. Whenever someone implied I needed to be more resilient, it felt like a subtle way of saying, 'you're failing. There's something wrong with you. Everyone else can suck it up and get on with it but you can't.' The problem with resilience is that we are taught to bounce back before we've even fallen.

It's very difficult to be resilient when your nervous system is stuck in a state of protection or dissociation. Trying to do a 180 and refocus on a positive when depressed or anxious is like trying to spin around with a piano on your back. The pace of the school routine needs slowing down for our children who are struggling to be resilient.

Guiding our children to identify and label their emotions and nervous system states needs to be balanced with a somatic-based approach to directly feel their emotions. The Zones of Regulation is a widely used program in schools, kindergartens and workplaces to foster self-regulation[28] and emotional control.[29] Offering daily classroom strategies to increase interoception *alongside* labelling emotions will give children the practical tools for lifelong mental health.

Interoception is a term to describe feeling your feelings. It is an internal sensory system where the internal physical and emotional states of the body are noticed, recognised, identified and responded to.[30] This skill needs explicit instruction to learn from an early age.

Developing a healthy relationship with our emotions is delicate. Classroom learning environments need to foster an acceptance of all emotions, without feeling shame about what might be perceived as having a 'bad' emotion. Self-connection can build our children's capacity to be authentic, value their own opinions, express their own needs and in turn, strengthen their mental and emotional health.

Children need support to learn that their bodies are working for them, not against them. Days before my son was to make his first appearance on stage for the local children's drama club, he told me he felt nervous. I asked him where he could feel the nerves in his body. He pointed to his chest as he exclaimed, 'Here!', while he jumped up and down with a shaky excitement. I asked him if he could gently pat the nerves in his chest and tell them they can be there. He did so and warmed to the idea of befriending his nerves rather than rejecting them.

On the night of Jackson's first performance, any actor's worst nightmare came true for him as he was struck with a severe case of stage fright, followed by big heaving cries, and he crawled into a ball on the floor of the stage. He forgot his lines and didn't know where he was meant to be positioned on stage. It took all my will to not run and save him but remain seated and watch from afar as his teacher held space for him. To my complete surprise, after a big hug with his teacher, some slow breaths, and time, he jumped back on stage and stole the show with the closing line of the scene.

Reflecting on his performance at bedtime that night, he felt proud of his performance and equally shameful of crying in a ball in front of everyone. I took the opportunity to explain that in that moment his body was helping him. I asked him how it felt to look out at all of the people who were watching him while he was on stage, and he replied, "scary!" I explained he got stage fright and it happens to lots of actors. I told him that his body helped him to keep safe from something so scary! He agreed and we ended the conversation in amazement at how smart our bodies are to do things to make sure we're safe and protected.

Not only can understanding their nervous systems and befriending their emotions help our children, simple movements work too. When my daughter Ivy is explosive with rage, I stretch my two palms out towards her so she can press her palms against mine. It gives her the proprioceptive input she needs to meet the sensations in her body. Plus, trying to push against me instantly turns into a playful game and her rage morphs into a fit of giggles.

When we learn to feel the perceived negative emotions, we learn to experience positive emotions too. Our ability to feel the full experience of pleasure, ecstasy, bliss and love makes a life worth living! Teaching interoception across all levels in schools will offer children vital skills to fall in love with life.

Children need role models to show them how it looks to feel their big feelings. When I am experiencing intense sensations in my body, I purposefully sit on the couch with a cup of tea and close my eyes while my children play around me. Sometimes I will cry and sometimes I won't. My children are used to this and often ask, "Mum, are you feeling your feelings?" And I'll simply reply, "yes".

Primary school-aged children need explicit guidance to practise applied mindfulness techniques like the Kiloby Inquiries to befriend their thoughts, nervous system states and emotions. The Australian Centre for Meditation and Mindfulness suggests that the age of the person practising mindfulness equals the number of minutes they can practise.

Children in the later years of primary school need open discussions about negative self-talk. They need practical steps to make friends with their negative thoughts so they're not overwhelmed by them or feel wrong for having them. As our children reach adolescence and experience more intense emotions, they need simple steps to find and process the root of their triggers.

Rather than focusing on controlling certain emotions and behaviours, we need to look for the root cause. In secondary school, I was disruptive in class when I didn't understand the work. I felt dumb because I didn't know how to do the work. Soon enough, I got bored and played up. Conversely, when a teacher sat with me to help me get started, I wasn't disruptive.

Let's shift our conversation away from *controlling* our emotions so we can avoid repressing our emotions.

It wasn't until recently that I understood what it means to control or *regulate* my emotions without repressing them. Firstly, I needed to learn how to feel safe to integrate decades of emotional baggage. Secondly, I needed to learn how to befriend my ever-changing nervous system states. Only then, could I regulate my emotions without repressing them. Deepening our direct and personal relationship with our own emotions will inform educational resources and steer mental health and emotional wellbeing in a healthier direction.

After two years of practising being present with my emotions, generally, when I put my direct attention on the sensations in my body rather than the story in my head, the sensations ease. It's like my presence with the nervous system and the corresponding sensation shaves the intensity off an emotion like anger and my body feels less explosive. It's like I am saying to my feelings 'it's okay, you're safe and I'm here'. This practice is the *opposite* of control, like taking my hands off the wheel and letting go. I return to a place of noticing my sensations, my emotions naturally stabilise and I come back to equilibrium.

Regulating my *attention* to my emotions is more vital than regulating my emotions. My recovery phase has had me focus on practising deep love, acceptance and awareness of the sensations derived from my nervous system. Regulating my attention by shifting it towards my emotions regulates both my emotions and my corresponding behaviour. By putting direct attention on the sensations in my body has me be at one with my emotions without doing or saying anything.

Changing the language from 'controlling' and 'regulating' our emotions to *befriending* our emotions is a great place to start. Befriending our emotions suggests that we are equal to our emotions and that they are not something to have power over and get rid of. This shifts the relationship we have with ourselves to one of companionship. This is the foundation for mental health.

When I was a classroom teacher, I didn't have time for my students' feelings. My students would often come in from lunchtime, worn out from running around in thirty-degree heat and humph themselves onto the carpet at my feet. At least one child would be upset with another because he pushed her or she wasn't letting him have a turn. They'd exchange expressions with each other that would slice through their soft, gentle brows like a knife. I wish I had the skills then, that I have now.

I couldn't deal with their little problems. I didn't have time. I had activities to get through, a messy classroom to pack up, and the thought of the leadership team breathing down my neck ensuring I was keeping up.

I had no time to spend on their feelings. When my students had big feelings, I would clench my teeth with frustration. My strategy was to solve the problem for them with adult rationality as quickly as possible so we could move on. Then I could get the afternoon activity done and I was one step closer to completing all required assessments to write end of semester reports. I dusted my hands off at the end of each year knowing my students achieved their learning outcomes.

But I saw in their eyes that they didn't feel heard. I didn't *hear* them. I didn't practise reflective listening or empathise with them for long. I didn't show them how to process their big feelings.

Children need safe spaces to learn how to process their anger, rage, panic and terror, through feeling. Feelings of panic and anger are signs that help us respond assertively to a situation that is unsafe. With interoception, our children can learn how to trust their bodies to guide them through life.

It's not the burnt-out teacher that needs to change, it's the pace of the education system. We are a sick society if we believe achieving learning outcomes is more important than our own health and wellbeing. Academic and career success becomes obsolete when mental illness takes over.

Practising oncologist and award-winning author of *A Better Death*, Dr Ranjana Srivastava describes suicide in the medical profession as common. In her book, she explained, 'the high rates of burnout, substance abuse and mental illness in the medical profession mean that many doctors know someone who has succumbed to a drug overdose or committed suicide.' She goes on to share, 'I have lost colleagues without having an inkling that there was something wrong with them – interns who didn't show up to work; specialists at the peak of their career; nurses who ran a ward just a week earlier.' Even the professionals we hold in the highest regard are falling prey to our societal imbalance.

I keep watching sacred sites being decimated and mountains of plastic killing tonnes of fish in the sea. Our sense of deficiency tells us we don't have time to stop, reconsider and create something new. We must keep going.

Deficiency driving education is felt in the undercurrent of anxiety-fuelled urgency and high pressure to keep pushing. This relentless force to do better and be better has led us to disconnect from our hearts and forget our basic needs to unite together and thrive.

To love.

What if we slowed down and let go of the things we think need doing? What if we halved the amount of tasks we completed each day and spent more time being present with the people in front of us? What would our world look like? How would our children feel? How would we feel? Imagine what life would feel like if we all felt heard, seen, and loved?

It's time to dream and rebuild a new world. A world built on collaboration, cooperation and where everyone benefits. And this can only happen when we all look within, integrate our emotions and realise we are not our deficiency stories.

Classrooms need to nurture our children's wild spirits, love of laughter and passion for life. Where we can fall, flip out from time to time, be in wild rage. Be human. Feel safe to express our unique selves. And dance more.

I healed my mental illness through letting go of control. I healed through learning how to safely feel the pain in my body, but also pleasure. I learnt how good it can feel when I put my attention on the sensations in my body when I dance and let my body move in the way it wants. Surrendering to my unique, fullest expression, had me fall madly in love with life.

Woodline Primary School, located just out of Geelong, Victoria, Australia, focuses on supporting and nurturing the whole child through emotional connection and awareness.[31] There are no more than sixteen students per classroom teacher. Small class sizes offer an opportunity for their students to feel heard and learn how to process their big feelings in the moment it arises, rather than storing it for later. Woodline Primary is a model for the future.

As parents and teachers, when we process our resistance to slow down and be patient with our children's feelings, we create space for new ways of interacting, living, learning and working. We build our capacity to hold space for ourselves and hold space for others. Then natural healing occurs for ourselves, each other, and our planet.

Greater connection with nature supports our mental health. We all know the mental fog we get when we stay inside, cooped up in a compact room with artificial light and stagnant air flow. And we know how refreshed, vibrant and alive we feel when we are in nature. We automatically co-regulate our nervous systems with nature. We can think clearly, we get great ideas, and we can hear our inner guidance.

Regular connection with nature helps our children thrive, grow and learn through play. My children and I feel invigorated when our hands are in the dirt, we're scrunching and smelling eucalyptus leaves, painting ourselves with clay and wrapping our arms around trees. It's time to revive an earth-honouring way of life so we experience the magic of deep connection with the land.

Teachers can guide their students to develop their interoceptive awareness in just a couple of minutes per day. Students need two 30-second interoception activities daily, coupled with explicit questions to connect with their bodies. They benefit from genuine demonstrations from their teacher showing them how to feel their feelings. And their teachers will benefit from knowing the latest neuroscience, the Velcro Effect and strategies to implement the Kiloby Inquiries in an age-appropriate way.

I am co-developing a school curriculum with a global team for children to learn the Kiloby Inquiries so they can move beyond emotional literacy and learn how to trust, feel and process the emotions in their bodies. When introduced to the Kiloby Inquiries for children, school teacher Susan shared: "this showed me there are other options to counselling for our students. I can see it's okay for students to feel their feelings and with these techniques it is achievable for them."

One of my youngest clients, at age 12, said the Kiloby Inquiries made her feel less stressed and like she was letting go of a lot of stuff. Modifying the Kiloby Inquiries for children to practise from a young age can strengthen their ability to befriend their negative thoughts and be with their feelings.

In order to create a world that fosters emotional connection, as parents and teachers, we need to take responsibility for the part we play. Simply being aware of how we are triggered by our children is essential to create a safe place for them to process their own big feelings.

Taking care of our own needs is the best step we can take for our children. Mini check-ins throughout the day, care and connection with ourselves is integral. When we feel tired, that's a sign the body is giving us to stop and rest. Your mind might tell you unhelpful stories that you need to push through. Look at those stories and then come to the body.

Our children are just waiting for us to be present. And through feeling our own feelings, we can find joy in simply being present with them. As a child, do you remember the magic of receiving love, care and attention from that one special person? That's all our kids want from us.

CHAPTER TEN
Integration

Safety is the presence of connection
- **Stephen Porges**

Mastering the techniques in this book may not take all of your triggers away. The ups and downs of life will inevitably still happen. In my case, the intensity of my worst days levelled out to something manageable and then beautiful. When you've got the tools to move everything through your system rather than have it stick and stay in your body and mind, life becomes easier and not something you need to escape.

Even though I know the beauty of practising, sometimes I still avoid it like the plague. But if I don't sit and feel the sensations in my body, they build up and latch onto every story that pops into my head. Sometimes I'll trick myself into thinking a run, massage or time with friends will suffice. But nothing works like being with the words, pictures and body sensations as they arise, from moment to moment.

When I don't practise the techniques, I feel antsy, annoyed and irritated by little things. I don't want to talk to anyone, and everything gets under my skin.

The best part is you can practise the Kiloby Inquiries anywhere, anytime. You don't have to be sitting alone in a room for it to work. You can look at the trigger words of a story on the wall while you eat breakfast. Then notice the sensations that are there in your body. You can put a picture of the person who has triggered you in the sky to look at as you go for a walk. Use all of the same techniques as you would if you were sitting down.

You don't have to wait until you're away from the person who's triggered you before you start processing your feelings. If you can, feel your feelings then and there. Then dive deeper with your journal beside you to clear the roots when you're alone later. While you're in conversation with them, see if you can hold your attention on your body sensations, the space around the two of you and what the person is saying. This is presence!

Being present takes slowing down. It takes time to notice if there is a scent in the air, to find the space around the person who's talking to you and to witness rising sensations in your body when someone's said something hurtful.

After looking at the same hurtful words in my mind many times, I began to see through them. I realised I wasn't the words. It was all smoke and mirrors.

The more I have learnt to lean into the feelings in my body, the more beauty I find within. At times, I notice every piece of every wave of emotion rise and fall. Sometimes holding conversations with others can become secondary when it feels so good to be connected with myself. What a contrast to those moments of not wanting to be alive.

My perplexed misunderstanding of self-connection and negative judgment on others for being loners has evolved into a deep love for being with myself. I am most content when I can feel my body sensations.

Before I knew how to be embodied, I lived from my mind. It was like leaving myself at the door of life to have surface-level interaction with the world. After engaging with others, I would fall in a heap afterwards and collect myself from the floor.

Now that I spend more time with myself, feeling my body's sensations, I take myself into conversations and relationships with others. I am present. And the more present I am for myself, the more available I become for others.

Escaping myself had me miss the most beautiful part of life. And finding immense beauty within me brought an unshakeable power too. Once I realised there was nothing to be frightened of within me, I wasn't afraid of looking inside of myself. I began to feel excited when I got triggered! When I got triggered, I could see what had been hidden, and it was on the way out.

I invite you to turn towards the trigger. Step back from mentally solving the problem and find out what deficiency story is driving it. Look at the words and pictures and then feel the body sensations. Gradually, you'll return to natural rest.

From natural rest you are a blank slate with no problems. From that place, you get to choose who you are, what you want, and then create it! Who do you want to be? How do you want to be in the world? How do you want to feel in your relationships? What do you want to create? How do you want to feel as you create it? You can be anything and create what you desire.

But be mindful. You can go charging ahead and quickly become successful from making big things happen from the mind's pushy slog and relentless orders. But where is the joy in that? Where are we experiencing pleasure in life when we are on a constant treadmill?

When we are creating what we desire while embodied, noticing how we are feeling, we're taking ourselves on the journey. We are alive and a part of life. We're noticing when things are off kilter, when we're triggered and process what's arising before we continue slowly.

Short practises can keep you embodied. Check in to see if your shoulders need dropping. Plant more weight into all edges of your feet. Keep it simple.

If you have resonated with this approach to dissolving depression, you might still feel some resistance. Maybe you think this isn't going to work, it sounds too hard and confusing, there's too much to look at or you're stuck with depression forever. These are all words.

In a nutshell, look at the words and pictures. Or feel the sensations in your body. Do one or the other. Doing both at the same time is what keeps us stuck.

If you don't feel like you're able to practise the techniques on your own yet, that's exactly how I started out. Your best next step is to be guided by a KI Facilitator. We won't rush you. We'll hold space for you as you master this work so you can feel clear, free, and at peace too.

Life is simply asking you to stay with yourself, be with yourself, and love all parts of yourself.

Thank you for taking this journey with me. It's taken twenty years to live life with depression and I am so thankful I'm on the other side. I cry with tears of relief, joy, pain, sorrow and freedom. There is deep satisfaction in my tears.

It's okay to cry. Let your body have your way with your emotions. Give yourself permission to cry.

Cry for all those times you didn't let yourself cry. Cry for all those times someone told you to stop. Cry for all those times no one could see that you were dying inside. Cry for all those times you were lonely and in despair. Just let yourself cry.

Feel the wet streaks down your cheeks. Let them drip to your jaw. Love them like precious diamonds. Watch how your tears subside on their own without you needing to stop them. Then feel your whole body release.

Give everyone around you permission to cry. Show them it's okay to cry too. Hold space for them. Hold space for them as you hold space for you.

Open your heart. Stay in your body. Feel all your feelings, whether you label them pain or pleasure. And feel the beauty of being you, just as you are.

Deep love from my heart to yours,

Bronte Spicer.

Acknowledgements

Thank you from the bottom of my heart. To my family for loving me all the way through, even when I couldn't feel it or see it. To Matt Nettleton for turning up at the right time. To Scott Kiloby and Dan McLintock for developing the techniques that changed my life. To Julianne Eanniello for nudging me deeper into my own KI practice. To Carlie Maree for kicking me into writing gear. To my KI clients for letting me witness your healing. To Amanda Spedding for refining my writing. To Ellie Schroeder for the exquisite cover art. To Debbie Hall for the powerful light codes. To my beta readers, friends and community for cheering me on. To Jackson, Ivy and Maggie for your genuine enthusiasm! And to Leigh for loving me from my rock-bottom through to my healing.

About The Author

Bronte Spicer is a teacher, author, mindfulness mentor, sacred space holder, intuitive guide and retreat alchemist. She shows people how to befriend their mind and feel their feelings so they can live the life they want, and thrive. Bronte is an award-winner writer at Elephant Journal and host to the podcast, 'It's Okay to Cry'. This is filled with conversations with real people using a body-based approach to improve their mental health. Whether you want to try a Kiloby Inquiries session, you're a teacher seeking classroom strategies to improve resilience in your students, or you want to boost staff wellbeing in your workplace, check out her website www.brontespicer.com.

ENDNOTES

1. Cognitive behaviour therapy (CBT), (2020) Cognitive behaviour therapy (CBT),. Available at: https://www.betterhealth.vic.gov.au/health/conditionsandtreatments/cognitive-behaviour-therapy (Accessed: 22/7/2021).

2. The History and Development of the Kiloby Inquiries (KI) can be found at https://kiloby.com/the-history-and-development-of-the-kiloby-inquiries-ki/ You can hear Scott explain the Kiloby Inquiries at https://www.youtube.com/watch?v=-qXJfUX12w4 You can watch me introduce Scott Kiloby and explain the Kiloby Inquiries here: https://www.youtube.com/watch?v=1W5eMh4Af_M&t=74s

3. Bessel A. van der Kolk and Onno van der Hart (1989) explain that a failure to arrange memories linguistically leaves it to be organized on a somatosensory or iconic level: as somatic sensations, behavioral re-enactments, nightmares, or flashbacks. Bessel A. van der Kolk, M.D., & Onno van der Hart, Ph.D., December 1989, 'Pierre Janet & the Breakdown of Adaptation in Psychological Trauma', American Journal of Psychiatry, 146 (12), 1530-1540, page 6. For further reading, read Van der Kolk BA, Ducey CR: The psychological processing of traumatic experience: Rorschach patterns in PTSD. J Traumatic Stress 1989; 2:259-274

4. YouTube. 2021. Deb Dana describes the Polyvagal Theory. - YouTube. [ONLINE] Available at: https://www.youtube.com/watch?v=JX-Gy7M4kvaY. [Accessed 08 September 2021].

5. nicabm-stealthseminar.s3.amazonaws.com. 2021. Limbic System Reverse Trauma's Physiological Imprint. [ONLINE] Available at: https://nicabm-stealthseminar.s3.amazonaws.com/Limbic+System/Reverse+Trauma's+Physiological+Imprint+Main+Session.pdf. [Accessed 07 August 2021]. (Traumatic) experiences then may be encoded on a sensori-motor level without proper localization in space and time. They therefore cannot be easily translated into the symbolic language necessary for linguistic retrieval. Pierre Janet & the Breakdown of Adaptation in Psychological Trauma Bessel A. van der Kolk, M.D., & Onno van der Hart, Ph.D. American Journal of Psychiatry, 146 (12), December 1989, 1530-1540.

6. The Weekend University, 2020, Polyvagal Theory and Trauma – Deb Dana, Available at: https://www.youtube.com/watch?v=M-SVdQ-CHkA, Accessed 22/7/21

   YouTube. 2021. Dr. Stephen Porges: What is the Polyvagal Theory - YouTube. [ONLINE] Available at: https://www.youtube.com/watch?v=ec3AUMDjtKQ. [Accessed 07 August 2021].

7. Nerd Nite (2017) The Polyvagal Theory: The New Science of Safety and Trauma. 4th November 2017 Available at https://www.youtube.com/watch?v=br8-qebjlgs 19:06 Accessed: 21 July 2021

8. Australian Institute of Health and Welfare, 2021 Deaths by Suicide over Time, Australian Government, viewed 22/7/21, https://www.aihw.gov.au/suicide-self-harm-monitoring/data/deaths-by-suicide-in-australia/suicide-deaths-over-time

9. www.blackdoginstitute.org.au. 2021. No page title. [ONLINE] Available at: https://www.blackdoginstitute.org.au/wp-content/uploads/2020/04/1-facts_figures.pdf?sfvrsn=8. [Accessed 28 July 2021].

10. Pierre Janet & the Breakdown of Adaptation in Psychological Trauma Bessel A. van der Kolk, M.D., & Onno van der Hart, Ph.D. American Journal of Psychiatry, 146 (12), December 1989, 1530-1540. Corresponding authors: Bessel van der Kolk, Psychiatry Department, Boston University Medical School, and Trauma Center at HRI Hospital, Brookline, Massachusetts, USA. Email: bvanderk@aol.com Onno van der Hart, Department of Clinical Psychology, Utrecht University, Heidelberg 1, 3584 CS Utrecht, The Netherlands. Phone: +31(30)253-1785; fax +31(30)253-4718; Email: o.vanderhart@fss.uu.nl

    Better Health Channel, 2021, Dissociation and dissociative disorders, Victorian Government, Available at: https://www.betterhealth.vic.gov.au/health/conditionsandtreatments/dissociation-and-dissociative-disorders (Accessed: 22/7/2021).

11. YouTube. 2021. TELUS Talks | Your body and mind are connected, with Dr. Gabor Maté - YouTube. [ONLINE] Available at: https://www.youtube.com/watch?v=jgN1UfgStxY. [Accessed 07 August 2021].

YouTube. 2021. When a Client Is Stuck in the Freeze Response with Peter Levine, PhD - YouTube. [ONLINE] Available at: https://www.youtube.com/watch?v=4Zsp4iRAGtc. [Accessed 28 July 2021].

12. The Weekend University, 2020, Polyvagal Theory and Trauma – Deb Dana, Available at: https://www.youtube.com/watch?v=M-SVdQ-CHkA, Accessed 22/7/21

13. Health and wellbeing. 2021. What is mindfulness? - Health and wellbeing. [ONLINE] Available at: https://www.monash.edu/health/mindfulness/what-is-mindfulness. [Accessed 28 July 2021].

14. YouTube. 2021. Polyvagal Theory and Trauma â Deb Dana - YouTube. [ONLINE] Available at: https://www.youtube.com/watch?v=M-SVdQ-CHkA. [Accessed 07 August 2021]., 43:33

15. YouTube. 2021. Polyvagal Theory and Trauma â Deb Dana - YouTube. [ONLINE] Available at: https://www.youtube.com/watch?v=M-SVdQ-CHkA. [Accessed 28 July 2021].

16. Chapter 4 from Porges SW & Dana D (2018). Clinical Applications of the Polyvagal Theory: The Emergence of Polyvagal-Informed Therapies. New York: WW Norton.YouTube. 2021. Polyvagal Theory and Trauma, Deb Dana - YouTube. [ONLINE] Available at: https://www.youtube.com/watch?v=M-SVdQ-CHkA. [Accessed 28 July 2021].

17. NICABM. 2021. Welcome to: Treating Trauma Master Series - NICABM. [ONLINE] Available at: https://www.nicabm.com/confirm/treating-trauma-master-2/. [Accessed 28 July 2021].

18. NICABM 2021. Treating Trauma Master Series Module 1 Main Session Neurobiology Trauma. [ONLINE] Available at: https://s3.amazonaws.com/nicabm-stealthseminar/Trauma2017/confirmed/NICABM-TreatingTraumaMasterSeries-Module1MainSession-NeurobiologyTrauma.pdf. [Accessed 07 August 2021].

19. www.ncbi.nlm.nih.gov. 2021. No page title. [ONLINE] Available at: https://www.ncbi.nlm.nih.gov/pmc/articles/PMC4316402/. [Accessed 05 August 2021].

    PART III – How Trauma Affects Memory and Recall - The Impact of Trauma on Adult Sexual Assault Victims. 2021. PART III – How Trauma Affects Memory and Recall - The Impact of Trauma on Adult Sexual Assault Victims. [ONLINE] Available at: https://www.justice.gc.ca/eng/rp-pr/jr/trauma/p4.html?fbclid=IwAR3AbseDhNfLIXWet_PICXq6Cs5rlSYnwTzoioGc1QyvMC04qP_HuU2ff5c. [Accessed 07 August 2021].

20. YouTube. 2021. 5 Types Of Unhealed Trauma - YouTube. [ONLINE] Available at: https://www.youtube.com/watch?v=GCeLbvEw_8w. [Accessed 05 August 2021].

21. YouTube. 2021. Gabor Mate - Trauma Is Not What Happens to You, It Is What Happens Inside You - YouTube. [ONLINE] Available at: http://www.youtube.com/watch?v=nmJOuTAk09g. [Accessed 28 July 2021].

22. www.ncbi.nlm.nih.gov. 2021. No page title. [ONLINE] Available at: https://www.ncbi.nlm.nih.gov/pmc/articles/PMC4316402/. [Accessed 05 August 2021].

    We behave as if the traumatic experience is still happening: "So we shall view memories as entities that predispose the mind to deal with new situations in old, remembered ways specifically, as entities that reset the states of parts of the nervous system. Then they can cause that nervous system to be predisposed to behave as though it remembers." Minsky M: K-lines: a theory of memory. Cognitive Science 1980; 4:117-133.

23. A., B., 2015. The Body Keeps the Score. Penguin Books.

24. Facebook. 2021. Log in to Facebook. [ONLINE] Available at: https://www.facebook.com/804324176356720/videos/773265139944188. [Accessed 28 July 2021].

25. Facebook. 2021. Log in to Facebook. [ONLINE] Available at: https://www.facebook.com/804324176356720/videos/773265139944188. [Accessed 28 July 2021].

26. How often do Australians cry? - ABC News. 2021. How often do Australians cry? - ABC News. [ONLINE] Available at: https://www.abc.net.au/news/2021-05-28/australia-talks-survey-asks-how-often-do-you-cry/13364494. [Accessed 28 July 2021].

27. Welcome to Head to Health | Head to Health. 2021. Welcome to Head to Health | Head to Health. [ONLINE] Available at: https://www.headtohealth.gov.au/. [Accessed 05 August 2021].

28. Raising Children Network. 2021. Self-regulation in children & teenagers | Raising Children Network. [ONLINE] Available at: https://raisingchildren.net.au/toddlers/behaviour/understanding-behaviour/self-regulation. [Accessed 05 August 2021].

29. THE ZONES OF REGULATION: A CONCEPT TO FOSTER SELF-REGULATION & EMOTIONAL CONTROL. 2021. THE ZONES OF REGULATION: A CONCEPT TO FOSTER SELF-REGULATION & EMOTIONAL CONTROL - Welcome. [ONLINE] Available at: https://www.zonesofregulation.com/index.html. [Accessed 05 August 2021].

30. https://www.education.sa.gov.au/schools-and-educators/curriculum-and-teaching/curriculum-programs/applying-interoception-skills-classroom?fbclid=IwAR3LH3GRQL8rTE0yIzoaKeubrwD28SK_917ghVTGrL-N8SI5re1dWaQUb1M. [Accessed 03 August 2021].

31. Woodline Primary. 2021. Woodline Primary | Fostering connection and awareness. [ONLINE] Available at: https://www.woodlineprimary.com.au/. [Accessed 05 August 2021].

www.ingramcontent.com/pod-product-compliance
Lightning Source LLC
Chambersburg PA
CBHW072010030526
44107CB00092B/2449